The Elements of
Technical Writing

The Elements of Composition Series

Series Editor: William A. Covino, Florida Atlantic University

The Elements of Technical Writing

Second Edition

Thomas E. Pearsall

Emeritus, University of Minnesota

Allyn and Bacon

Boston   London   Toronto   Sydney   Tokyo   Singapore

Vice President: *Eben Ludlow*
Editorial Assistant: *Grace Trudo*
Marketing Manager: *Christopher Bennem*
Editorial-Production Service: *Susan Freese, Communicáto, Ltd.*
Text Design and Electronic Composition: *Denise Hoffman*
Composition and Prepress Buyer: *Linda Cox*
Manufacturing Buyer: *Suzanne Lareau*
Cover Administrator: *Jenny Hart*

Library of Congress Cataloging-in-Publication Data

Pearsall, Thomas E.
    The elements of technical writing / Thomas E. Pearsall. — 2nd ed.
        p.   cm.— (Elements of composition series)
    Includes bibliographical references and index.
    ISBN 0–205–31873–8
    I. Technical writing.   I. Title.   II. Series

    T11.P39   2000
    808'.0666—dc21   00-030603

Printed in the United States of America

10 9 8 7 6 5 4 3   05 04 03 02

Contents

Part Two
The Formats of Technical Writing 77

Preface

Technical writing, purely and simply, is writing about subjects in technical disciplines. Whether agriculture, economics, engineering, or zoology, a technical discipline will have its *technics*—that is, its theories, principles, arts, and skills. It will generate reports and correspondence. The hallmark of such reports and correspondence is that they present objective data to *convince,* rather than emotion to *persuade.*

People in every technical discipline will propose research, report progress on research, and report the results of the research. In addition, people will instruct, transmit information, and argue for the validity of their opinions. Such is the stuff of technical writing, and such is the stuff of this book.

Plan of the Book

This second edition contains seven chapters on the principles of technical writing and three on the formats—ten chapters in all. To help readers tie everything together, four appendixes demonstrate typical technical reports and correspondence.

The seven chapters in Part One present the essential principles of good technical writing:

- Chapter 1, Know Your Purpose
- Chapter 2, Know Your Audience
- Chapter 3, Organize Your Content around Your Purpose and Audience
- Chapter 4, Write Clearly and Precisely
- Chapter 5, Use Good Page Design
- Chapter 6, Think Visually
- Chapter 7, Write Ethically

Part Two covers some of the structural and organizational features of technical writing:

- Chapter 8, Elements of Reports, describes such elements as title pages, abstracts, introductions, and documentation.
- Chapter 9, Formats of Reports, provides formats for major reports, such as research reports, recommendation reports, and proposals.
- Chapter 10, Formats of Correspondence, shows how to format letters and memorandums and how to write letters ofapplication and résumés.

The four appendixes provide illustrative samples of the following:

- A letter analytical report
- A student proposal
- A progress report
- An empirical research report

Changes in the Second Edition

The changes made in this edition reflect the ever-changing nature of technical writing and address comments received from reviewers of the previous edition:

- Many new and more technical examples have been drawn from the fields of engineering (civil, mechanical, nuclear, and environmental), chemistry, biology, geology, and meteorology.
- Advice has been provided on constructing outlines; a sample outline has been included, as well.
- Documentation guidelines for Internet materials have been added based on the *Columbia Guide to Online Style*.
- The discussion of e-mail has been expanded.
- The section on résumés now includes advice on preparing digital and scannable résumés.
- The appendixes have been improved to include new examples of a student proposal and progress report based on environmental engineering and a new empirical research report from forest science.

Acknowledgments

I have, in many places, acknowledged the sources of ideas and materials. Most often, the ideas have come from a combination of places that would be impossible to document. They are the materials that those of us in technical writing have freely shared with each other for years. But I would be remiss if I did not acknowledge here some of the people who have shaped my thoughts the most: Paul Anderson, Virginia Book, W. Earl Britton, David Carson, Mary Coney, Donald Cunningham, Sam Dragga, Herman Estrin, Jay Gould, John Harris, Ken Houp, Ann Laster, Fred MacIntosh, Victoria Mikelonis, John Mitchell, Nell Ann Pickett, Janice Redish, Tom Sawyer, Jim Souther, Elizabeth Tebeaux, John Walter, Tom Warren, Arthur Walzer, and Mike White. Blessings on them all, and double blessings on anyone I have neglected to mention.

I also thank my colleagues who reviewed the previous edition of this book for Allyn and Bacon and made many useful suggestions for this new edition: Carolyn Plumb, University of Washington; Norma Procopiow, University of Maryland; and Ricky W. Telg, University of Florida. And once again, I thank those individuals who reviewed the manuscript of the first edition: Dan Jones, University of Central Florida, and Art Walzer, University of Minnesota.

Finally, I thank my invaluable editor of many years, Eben Ludlow.

T. E. P.

PART ONE

The Seven Principles of Technical Writing

1

Know Your Purpose

What goal do you have in writing? What objective do you wish to achieve? What result do you hope for? What do you want to accomplish? In short, all these questions address what you see as your *purpose* in whatever it is you are writing, whether an e-mail message, a résumé, or a major report. Basically, technical writing has only two purposes: (1) to inform and (2) to argue. Given that, consider these two examples of purpose:

> To inform mechanical engineers about the sturdy foam metals becoming available in the marketplace
>
> To inform mechanical engineers about the sturdy foam metals becoming available in the marketplace and to argue for the superiority of foam metal over solid metal in certain applications

The first purpose—to inform—will be met by writing a report that objectively describes the foam metals becoming available. The report that satisfies the second purpose—to argue—should be no less objective but will contain an argument that evaluates the solids and the foams to demonstrate the superiority claimed. For example, the argument might compare and contrast the solids and the foams in certain applications. (See Chapter 9 for various formats used in informing and arguing.)

Many variations on reports that inform and argue exist in technical writing. For instance, definitions and descriptions are largely informative. So are written instructions, for the most part, although argument may play a role, as in this example:

> This new way of dry cleaning is more environmentally friendly than the old way.

But much of technical writing is argumentative. Research reports inform their readers of the facts that have been uncovered and then argue for the reliability of the conclusions drawn from those facts. Similarly, recommendation reports inform, analyze, evaluate, and draw conclusions that support their recommendations. Proposals argue for engaging an organization to do a certain task. And so on.

To succeed as a writer, you must clearly envision your purpose for whatever it is you are writing. You are more likely to succeed in achieving your purpose if you state it in writing:

> I want to convince the executives of Elmont Bank to accept my company's proposal to update the software used by their tellers in reporting bank transactions.

> I want to demonstrate to the upper management of Dickens' Sporting Goods Company the feasibility of using titanium foam in the manufacture of golf club heads.

> My purpose is to instruct the tellers of Elmont Bank how to use the new software we have installed for their use in reporting bank transactions.

> My purpose is to explain to the technicians who manufacture golf clubs for Dickens' Sporting Goods Company the techniques required for working with titanium foam.

Notice that all these statements of purpose identify to whom the report is directed, that is, to what *audience*. Understanding your audience is as essential to producing a successful piece of writing as understanding your purpose. We explore the concept of audience in the next chapter, Know Your Audience.

2

Know Your Audience

Good writers are aware of their audiences. As you visualize your readers, consider these things:

- Their concerns and characteristics
- Their levels of education and experience
- Their attitudes toward your purpose and information

Concerns and Characteristics

Figure 2.1 summarizes the concerns and characteristics of five major audiences you may face as a technical writer and indicates some ways to satisfy the needs of each. For example, notice that executives read primarily for the purpose of making decisions. Thus, an executive will be disappointed by a report that does not clearly state the author's conclusions and back up those conclusions with sufficient but succinct information. Notice also that executives read selectively, skimming and scanning materials. Picture an officer in a large company, facing a desk piled high with reports. Looking over these reports, the officer can make various judgments and exercise options accordingly:

Audience	Concerns and Characteristics
Laypersons	• Read for learning and interest • Have more interest in practice than theory • Need help with science and mathematics • Enjoy and learn from human interest • Require background and definitions • Need simplicity • Learn from simple graphics
Executives	• Read to make decisions • Have more interest in practice than theory • Need plain language • Learn from simple graphics • Need information on people, profits, and environment • Expect implications, conclusions, and recommendations expressed clearly • Read selectively—skimming and scanning • Have self-interests as well as corporate interests
Technicians	• Read for how-to information • Expect emphasis on practical matters • May have limitations in mathematics and theory • May expect theory if higher level
Experts	• Read for how and why things work • Need and want theory • Will read selectively • Can handle mathematics and terminology of field • Expect graphics to display results • Need new terms defined • Expect inferences and conclusions to be clearly but cautiously expressed and well supported
Combined	• One person may combine the attributes of several audiences • Readers may consist of representatives of several audiences

FIGURE 2.1   Audience Concerns and Characteristics

> This entire report directly concerns decisions I have to make; I need to read it carefully and evaluate the information and conclusions presented.

> Some of this report concerns my department; I better look through it and read the pertinent parts carefully.

> This report looks interesting; I better scan it.

> This report contains nothing of concern to me; I will initial and pass it on.

Using the information in this book about good page design (see Chapter 5) and formats of technical writing (see Part Two), you can support executives' thinking processes and allow them to read selectively.

Unlike executives, technicians read primarily for how-to information. For example, you operate as a technician when you consult the instruction manual for, say, your personal computer. You go to that manual to learn how to operate the computer or perhaps to solve a particular problem you are having with it. And you expect the information in the manual to be written in language you clearly understand and organized in a format you can easily access.

In similar fashion, experts read professional books, journals, and papers to keep up to date on the latest research and developments in their fields and to guide their work, and laypeople read things that may interest or entertain them or influence their attitudes and decisions. Keeping your readers' concerns and characteristics in mind is essential to satisfying their needs and to accomplishing your own purpose.

Education and Experience

Based on our individual levels of education and experience, we all learn *vocabulary, concepts,* and *techniques* for doing things. For example, civil engineers understand that the term *safety factor* means "the margin by which a machine exceeds its required performance." The safety factor for most passenger elevators is 7.6; that is, they will carry 7.6 times the average weight of the number of passengers they are specified to carry. In addition, engineers understand the concept of *safety factor.* They could build elevators with a safety factor of 30, but the cost would be so excessive that no one could afford it. Therefore, safety factors are based on a balance of safety and cost.

When civil engineers write, they have to know which technical engineering terms and concepts their readers will likely know and not know. When writing for fellow engineers, they can assume a shared vocabulary and understanding and leave technical terms and concepts undefined and unexplained. When writing for nonengineers, however, they will have to define and explain as necessary, based on the audience's level of education and experience.

Similarly, through education and experience, we learn techniques for doing things. Consider that the technical writers who produced the computer manual you use had to estimate your knowledge of how to use a keyboard and mouse. If they estimated correctly, you will be a happy reader; if their judgment was incorrect, you will be an unhappy reader.

When you write about what you have learned through your own education and experience, you must consider how well your readers will understand the words, concepts, and techniques you write about. Accordingly, when you think your readers might need help with any of these aspects, offer it.

Attitudes toward Purpose and Information

Consider these possible situations:

> You are writing a report for your supervisor that recommends the purchase of a new, more powerful computer for the office in which the two of you work. You know that your supervisor wants to buy the computer and is looking for support to justify the purchase.

Or maybe the reverse is true:

> Your supervisor does not think the new computer is needed. In fact, she considers it a waste of money.

In the first situation, your supervisor will read your report in a happy frame of mind. If she has the sole decision-making authority to buy the computer, she may not even read the entire report carefully. Your supervisor's approach to your report will be different, however, if she needs to convince someone higher up the chain of command to buy the computer. She will still be happy with your report but will perhaps read it with more care to make sure your argument convincingly expresses your purpose: to justify purchase of the new computer.

In the second situation, your supervisor will be at least skeptical of both your purpose and your information; she may even be hostile. As such, she will read carefully, looking for flaws and weaknesses in your argument for buying the computer. It will take a strong, well-supported argument to convince her.

Consider the position of someone writing technical instructions. He must acknowledge that few people approach technical instructions with joy in their hearts. Instead, they most likely want to use the instructions to find what information they need and to do so as quickly and easily as possible. Readers with this attitude want to read instructions selectively; that is, they want to read only those parts they need and skip the rest.

Suppose, for example, you are writing online instructions about how to use a software program that calculates and reports federal income tax. What kinds of information will your readers want? All of them will want to know two basic things: (1) how to load the software into their computers and (2) how to complete a standard 1040 tax form.

Beyond those two skills, however, individual readers will have different needs. For instance, some may need to know how to deal with child-support payments, home-office expenses, or individual retirement accounts (IRAs). Others may need to know how to transfer information from other programs into the tax program or vice versa.

Whatever the specific interest, no one wants to read through unneeded information to get to needed information. Being forced to do so will put anyone in a hostile mood. Therefore, in writing instructions, or any technical document, ensure that it is organized and designed to be read selectively.

As these examples indicate, people can approach reading technical documents with widely varying attitudes: agreement or hostility, trust or skepticism, passion or indifference, eagerness or reluctance. One attitude, however, is nearly universal: No one wants to linger. In our busy world, readers want to find what they need in a piece of technical writing, comprehend it, and move on. When writing a technical document, your job is to help them do just that.

3

Choose and Organize Your Content around Your Purpose and Audience

If you follow the advice given in Chapters 1 and 2 about purpose and audience, you will find it easier to choose your content and organize your report. Make sure you clearly understand the following:

- Your purpose
- Your reader's or readers' concerns and characteristics
- Your reader's or readers' education and experience in the subject area
- Your reader's or readers' attitudes toward your purpose

Because good writing is precise, for a lengthy, important piece of writing, it is a good idea to write down this information, something like this:

Purpose: My purpose is to write a brochure for the members of a health maintenance organization (HMO) that explains the role of folic acid in preventing neural tube malformations (anencephaly and spina bifida) and how women of childbearing age can ensure they get sufficient folic acid in their diets to prevent such malformations during pregnancy.

Readers' concerns and characteristics: The audience I wish to reach, either directly or through relatives or friends, is women of childbearing age. Essentially, this will be an audience of laypeople who read for learning and interest. My readers probably have some concerns about good health and healthy babies, but because they don't know the dangers of neural tube malformations, they have no concerns about them. This audience will require background information and definitions along with graphics and an easy-to-read text.

Readers' education and experience in the subject area: Because a wide cross-section of U.S. society belongs to HMOs, my readers likely have an average level of education (certainly no higher than high school and perhaps as low as the eighth grade). This means I should assume that my readers have no clear knowledge of the role of folic acid in the diet or what neural tube birth malformations are.

Readers' attitudes toward my purpose: Because many people do not worry about health problems until they actually appear, I should assume a certain amount of reader indifference toward my purpose.

When you have completed this analysis, you are ready to choose your content and to organize it in the way that best suits your purpose and audience.

Choosing Content

The principle you should follow in choosing content is a simple one: *Choose the level and amount of content that is needed to fulfill your purpose and your readers' needs—but no more than that.*

Even though this principle seems simple, it is not easy to follow. Most writers—particularly those who are experts in the subjects they are writing about—tell readers more than they really want to know. For example, most owners of VCRs do not care to know anything about VCRs except how to set them and use them. Giving readers additional information is more than a waste of time. It may actually get in the way of the information that they really do need.

On the other hand, experts in a scientific field reading a report of an experiment in their field probably want information that would not concern or interest nonexperts. Likewise, to be credible and convincing in an argument, you have to provide sufficient information to demonstrate that your conclusions are probably correct.

In other words, choosing content requires thought and judgment on your part. It requires putting yourself in your readers' place. Perhaps the best way to do that is to ask the questions that readers might have. Looking at the HMO example again will illustrate the process.

Imagine for a moment that you are one of the readers of the HMO brochure about folic acid and neural tube malformations. You may be a woman of childbearing age, or perhaps you have friends or relatives who fall into that group. What do you want to know? Your list might include these questions:

What are neural tube malformations?

Will folic acid prevent neural tube malformations?

How much folic acid is required?

When do I need to take folic acid?

Why are neural tube malformations dangerous?

Who is in danger?

What foods or food supplements will provide a sufficient supply of folic acid?

You should choose content that will answer such questions for your readers. Choose enough content so that your answers will be credible and convincing, but do not overload your readers with too much technical detail. For instance, to answer the last question on the list, tell your readers that foods containing folic acid include dark-green leafy vegetables, fruits, beans, whole grains, and breakfast cereals. Indicate, perhaps in a table, how much folic acid each of these foods contains. In addition, tell your readers that most all-purpose vitamin pills contain folic acid. Use a similar method in choosing the content needed to answer the other questions.

Organizing Your Content

When *organizing* your content, as when *choosing* it, keep your readers' needs firmly in mind. In the HMO example, the questions raised suggest that the brochure will be issue or topic oriented. That is, it will give information about specific topics within the general subject of folic acid and neural tube malformations. Many informative reports present a major topic divided into several subtopics, like this:

Topic	*Exposure to insecticides*
Subtopic 1	Exposure through food
Subtopic 2	Exposure through water
Subtopic 3	Exposure through air
and so on	

In the HMO example, the answers to the questions will be the topics and subtopics for the brochure. How to arrange them still needs to be decided. Your audience analysis told you that most of your readers will not know what neural tube birth malformations are. This suggests that you should first define the term. Definitions grow out of the scheme for a logical definition:

term = genus or class + differentia

In other words, begin your definition by identifying what general class or category your subject belongs to and then provide details to fine-tune your description. For example:

Neural tube malformations are serious birth defects that cause disability or death. They are the most common disabling birth defects, affecting between 1 and 2 out of every 1,000 births in the United States.

There are two main kinds of neural tube malformations: anencephaly and spina bifida. A baby with anencephaly does not develop a brain and dies shortly after birth. Spina bifida is a malformation of the spinal column. If the vertebrae (i.e., bones of the spinal column) surrounding the spinal cord do not close properly during the first 28 days of fetal development, the cord or spinal fluid will bulge through, usually in the lower back.[1]

Look at the first sentence, which follows the scheme for a logical definition:

Neural tube malformations *(term)* are serious birth defects *(genus)* that cause disability or death *(differentia).*

This definition is then extended with additional information, such as statistics and descriptions; graphic illustrations could be added, as well. Remember, however, that you should not add more detail than your purpose and your readers' needs require.

After you have told your readers what neural tube malformations are, what do you do next? Look at your questions again:

What are neural tube malformations?

Will folic acid prevent neural tube malformations?

How much folic acid is required?

When do I need to take folic acid?

Why are neural tube malformations dangerous?

Who is in danger?

What foods or food supplements will provide a sufficient supply of folic acid?

Next, it would seem to be a good idea to emphasize just how dangerous spina bifida is and who is in danger by describing some of the disabilities involved and adding graphic illustrations of some of them. After you have made a convincing case regarding the dangers of spina bifida, you could then answer the questions concerning folic acid as a preventive measure that all women of childbearing age should follow. The questions concerning folic acid would lend themselves to being organized as a series of subtopics under one topic, like this:

Will folic acid prevent neural tube malformations?

When do I need to take folic acid?

How much folic acid is required?

What foods or food supplements will provide a sufficient supply of folic acid?

Laypeople follow topical discussions well if you use the questions that generated the topics as your organizing device and the actual questions as topic headings. Therefore, your final organizational outline for the brochure might look like this:

What are neural tube malformations?

Why are neural tube malformations dangerous?

Will folic acid prevent neural tube malformations?

When do I need to take folic acid?

How much folic acid is required?

What foods or food supplements will provide a sufficient supply of folic acid?

Although every topical organizational plan grows out of answers to questions, you need not use questions as headings in every situation. For example, for a more expert audience, question-type headings might be inappropriate. But for lay audiences, question-type headings often are the best approach.

You have many organizational schemes available. You may use one of them to organize your entire report and others to organize sections or even paragraphs within it. Here, briefly explained, are some of the most common organizational schemes.

Chronological

In a *chronological* scheme, information is organized by time. You should choose this scheme to report a sequence of events or explain the steps in a process. The following example shows a sequence of events in the order in which they happened:

Event 1   The accident

Event 2   The investigation

Event 3   The trial

and so on

Chronology is also a major organizing pattern in process descriptions:

Step 1   Design the product

Step 2   Build the prototype

Step 3   Test the prototype

Classification and Division

In *classification,* you work from the specific to the general, seeking classifications (that is, categories) for items. For example, your knowledge of house windows might tell you that their frames are made of various materials, such as aluminum, wood, vinyl, and fiberglass. Therefore, in writing about windows, you might find it convenient to classify them by their framing materials. In *division,* you work from the general to the specific. That is, you might start with the generalization *house windows* and divide by *framing materials.*

Whether you start at the bottom with specifics or at the top with a generalization, the result is the same: a classification and a set of items that belong in it. For example:

House windows
  Aluminum
  Wood
  Vinyl
  Fiberglass

Be sure that every equal classification or division is based on the same principle. That is, in a classification scheme based on window frame materials, do not introduce another equal classification based on durability. It would be appropriate, however, to create subclassifications based on such things as durability, cost, and efficiency:

House windows
  Aluminum
    Durability
    Cost
    Efficiency

Keep your purpose and audience in mind when choosing a classification scheme. For instance, suppose you are classifying *insecticides.* For chemists, it might be most appropriate to classify insecticides by their chemical properties; however, for farmers, it might be best to classify according to the types of insects the insecticides control. You could classify *cities* in literally thousands of ways: by location; racial/ethnic mix; population; numbers of hotels and restaurants; type of government; availability, number, and size of convention rooms; and so forth. For convention planners, classification schemes based on the numbers of restaurants, hotels, and convention rooms might best serve their interests.

Mechanism Descriptions

Descriptions of mechanisms are common in technical writing. You will find many examples of them in technical advertisements, empirical research reports, and instructions. As always, the amount of detail presented should be based on your purpose, your readers' concerns and characteristics, your readers' level of knowledge and experience in the area, and your readers' attitudes toward your purpose. But in general, mechanism descriptions follow a three-part scheme. Here's an example, explaining a mechanism called a *scarifier*, which is used to prepare forest floors for the regeneration of trees:

1. **Overview**	The modified drag-chain is designed to be pulled by crawler-tractors in the 30- to 50-horsepower class. The modified drag-chain scarifier was designed to expose mineral soil in spot areas under standing trees. Preliminary tests indicate that the modified chain may distribute seed better than rakes or disks, although rakes and disks may provide better soil disturbance.
2. **Division into component parts and description of the parts**	The modified drag-chain employs two lengths of lightweight drag-chain instead of the three heavy strands in the original. Two-inch-square bar stock, 24 inches long, welded to each length of chain, increases scarification. . . .
3. **Mechanism in action**	The chain is self-cleaning and rolls over slash downfall better than other implements. Roots of competing grasses are pulled out by the chain. . . .[2]

Mechanism descriptions are generally accompanied by graphic illustrations, such as drawings and photographs (discussed further in Chapter 6).

Because similar situations occur so often in technical writing, many useful formats and organizational plans have been developed. You can often use such plans and formats, perhaps in modified forms, to choose and organize content in your writing. Part Two, The Formats of Technical Writing, will provide a lot of useful information on choosing and organizing content. Chapter 9, in particular, on formats of reports, will give you detailed accounts of how to write instructions, analytical reports, proposals, progress reports, and empirical research reports.

Knowing the basic formats and uses of these organizational schemes will help you organize a piece of writing. But nothing is as important as choosing your content and organizing it around your purpose and audience. In the HMO brochure example, knowledge of your purpose and audience should have led you to organize your writing by topic, even if you had never heard of topical arrangement.

Outlines

Make an outline when you are organizing. Writing things down helps clarify your thoughts. Things not written down may be forgotten. Trying to write something down and not being able to express it clearly may suggest to you that it's the wrong approach. You do not necessarily need to make a formal outline full of roman numerals and capital letters. But you should keep a good record of your organization with an informal outline of headings and subheadings. When you have a coherent outline that matches your purpose and audience, you will be ready to write.

Should you need a formal outline, carefully follow the format in Figure 3.1, which illustrates a typical topic outline. In outlines, the letters and numbers that serve as labels alternate, like this:

I.
  A.
    1.
      a.
        (1)
          (a)
          (b)
        (2)
      b.
    2.
  B.
II.

Solar Water Heating

Before considering installing a solar water heater, homeowners should understand the components and types of solar water heaters currently available, how to estimate the size of the system they need, and the economic and environmental benefits of installed systems.

I. Solar water heater components
   A. Collectors
      1. Flat-plate collectors
      2. Evacuated-tube collectors
      3. Concentrating collectors
   B. Storage tanks
   C. Pumps
II. Types of solar water heaters
   A. Active systems
      1. Open-loop systems
         a. Advantages
         b. Disadvantages
      2. Closed-loop systems
         a. Advantages
         b. Disadvantages
   B. Passive systems
      1. Batch heaters
         a. Advantages
         b. Disadvantages
      2. Thermosiphon systems
         a. Advantages
         b. Disadvantages
III. System size
IV. Benefits of solar water heaters
   A. Economic benefits
      1. Florida Solar Energy Center analysis
      2. Paybacks
   B. Environmental benefits

FIGURE 3.1 Topic Outline

Source: Adapted from *Solar Water Heating* (Washington, DC: U.S. Department of Energy, 1996).

Notice that the logic of an outline requires that you have a *II* when you have a *I*, a *B* when you have an *A*, and so on through the outline. As in Figure 3.1, begin your outline with a statement that clearly indicates your purpose and audience.

4

*Write Clearly
and Precisely*

When you write the first draft of a document, do it rapidly and without much regard for mechanics and style. Using the content and organization you have arrived at (by following the guidelines in Chapters 1 through 3), get your information out where you can see it. Writing is thinking, so often, while writing, you will see different ways of organizing and different content choices. Follow the flow of your writing. Don't be a slave to organizational plans.

When you have completed your first draft, check its content and organization once again to be sure you have met your purpose and your audience's needs. Revise, if necessary. When you have done that, then it is time to make sure that your paragraphing, sentence structure, and language present your content clearly and precisely.

Paragraph for Readers

Imagine reading page after page of prose without any paragraphs. They would appear dense and forbidding. Therefore, the first principle of paragraphing is to *paragraph often*, so you don't frighten off your readers. Judging by standard practice in well-written prose, paragraphs of

60 to 100 words seem about right, depending in part on the page design. For example, letters or pages that are formatted in narrow columns will likely have shorter paragraphs than standard report pages.

In technical writing, the first sentence in a paragraph generally introduces its subject and frequently provides a transition from the previous paragraph. You don't need to be heavy handed about either the introduction or the transition. These few paragraphs illustrate how to introduce the topic in the first paragraph and then move on to subtopics in subsequent paragraphs:

> The three major causes of land degradation are destructive agricultural practices, deforestation, and overgrazing.
>
> Destructive agricultural practices and land mismanagement account for 27 percent of the world's soil degradation, much of it in North America. Soil has been lost by repeated use of conventional tillage with heavy equipment and failure to use contour plowing on sloping terrain. Since 1930, the U.S. Government has spent $18 billion in conservation measures to reduce soil erosion. Despite present expenditures of $1 billion a year, the U.S. still annually loses some 6 billion tons of topsoil.
>
> Land degradation is especially acute in the former Soviet Union, a consequence of short-sighted industrial agricultural practices that ignored natural factors and faith that technology, fertilizers, and pesticides could increase crop yields interminably. Of Russia's 13.6 million acres of irrigated land, one-fifth is too salinized and two-fifths too acidified to support production. . . .
>
> Deforestation exposes fragile tropical soils to rainfall. . . .
>
> Overgrazing causes 35 percent of desertification, the most prevalent type of soil degradation. . . .[1]

The first one-sentence paragraph serves as a transition from the previous subject by announcing that the new subject will be *the three major causes of land degradation*. The first sentence in the second paragraph makes the transition to *destructive agricultural practices in North America*. The rest of the paragraph provides some supporting data.

The first sentence of the third paragraph lets you know that *land degradation* is still the subject but the focus has shifted to the former

Soviet Union, and so on. The fourth paragraph, on *deforestation,* makes the transition to the new subject simply by beginning *Deforestation exposes . . .* The transition to *overgrazing* is made with the paragraph beginning *Overgrazing causes . . .*

The writer shifts gears between subjects simply by using key terms. The writer also keeps the reader's eyes on the subject by repeating key terms. Notice how many times *degradation* occurs in the sample paragraphs. (For that matter, notice how many times the words *paragraph* and *paragraphs* occur in this section discussing paragraphs.)

Not repeating key terms—or worse, using variant terms (for example, *deterioration* for *degradation*)—may cause your readers to lose sight of the subject or think a shift in subject has occurred. Don't be afraid to use intelligent repetition.

Use Language Appropriate for Your Readers

When you have done your audience analysis, you should have a good idea of the language level you can use. For instance, you will not want to throw terms from physics, sociology, or agronomy at readers who are not knowledgeable in those fields. On the other hand, for experts in these areas, more sophisticated language would be appropriate and even expected.

Here, for example, are a few sentences aimed at readers who are presumed to be knowledgeable about the words and concepts of molecular biophysics. For the intended audience, the language used is entirely appropriate. For other readers, however, at least several of the words and concepts presented will cause difficulty:

> To what degree do the mechanics of soluble protein motions apply to membrane proteins? Helices in membrane proteins are believed to be as tightly packed as those in soluble proteins. This crucial fact, which implies that the constraints on soluble also apply to membrane proteins, is borne out by calculations showing that the buried atoms in membrane proteins occupy the same (or even less) space as comparable atoms in soluble proteins.[2]

Notice the difference in the language used in the next illustration, which is from a publication of the American Heart Association. This text is clearly aimed at intelligent but uninformed readers:

> When a heart attack occurs, the dying part of the heart may trigger electrical activity that causes *ventricular fibrillation.* This is an uncoordinated twitching of the ventricles that replaces the smooth, measured contractions that pump blood to the body's organs. Many times if trained medical professionals are immediately available, they can use electrical shock to start the heart beating again.
>
> If the heart can be kept beating and the heart muscle is not too damaged, small blood vessels may gradually reroute blood around blocked arteries. This is how the heart compensates; it's called *collateral circulation.*

For the most part, the American Heart Association sample uses simple, everyday words, such as *trigger, twitch,* and *blocked.* The two technical terms used—*ventricular fibrillation* and *collateral circulation*—are well defined.

Inflated language is never appropriate for any audience. Resist the temptation to impress your readers with fancy and pompous words. Choose simple, common words as much as possible. Don't *utilize* things; *use* them. Don't *initiate* and *terminate* things; *start* and *stop* them. Avoid phrases like *due to the fact that* and *at the present time;* simple words like *because* and *now* will serve you and your readers better.

Prefer the Active Voice

Active-voice sentences clearly state who or what the actor is and what the actor is doing. For that reason, most readers find sentences written in the active voice easier to follow and understand than those written in the passive voice. In addition, sentences written in the active voice seem more direct and interesting. You should use the active voice for the bulk of your writing.

In active-voice sentences, the subject acts in some way. For example:

> The director reported that the spacecraft will begin mapping operations earlier than expected.

Phase I of the program runs until June.

The proposal includes two missions for 2002.

Notice that the subject does not have to be a person. As shown in these examples, the subject can be a *phase,* a *proposal*—anything at all.

In a passive-voice sentence, the subject is acted upon:

The ultraviolet emissions were detected by several astronomers.

Satellites, such as the earth's moon, are bound to their planets by the pull of gravity.

It is all too easy in a passive-voice sentence to omit the final prepositional phrase (beginning with *by*) that identifies the actor, even when that knowledge may be important. For example:

New technology was developed to revolutionize high-speed air travel.

To rewrite this sentence in the active voice requires adding an actor—who or what developed the new technology:

NASA developed new technology to revolutionize high-speed air travel.

Passive voice does have a place. When the identity of the actor is obvious or irrelevant (as is often the case in the "Materials and Methods" section of a research report), use the passive voice:

Relative air moisture (percent) in the tunnel house was recorded using 2 HMP35C probes (Campbell Scientific) installed 2 m (6.6 ft) from the soil. A data logging system (Campbell Scientific Model CR-10) was programmed to compile data obtained from a probe every 5 minutes and to calculate hourly averages. Mean daily and monthly moisture levels were determined by a program developed using SAS software.[3]

Use the passive voice when it's appropriate, but prefer the active voice on most occasions. Your readers will appreciate it.

Use Personal Pronouns

Personal pronouns go hand in hand with the active voice. If the author or authors of a report wish to express an opinion or relate an action, it's appropriate to write an active-voice sentence that begins with *I* or *we*, as in:

> I recommend the opening of the new office in Dayton as soon as possible.

Not to use *I* in this sentence would result in a bloodless passive-voice sentence:

> The opening of a new office in Dayton is recommended by the author.

The following would be even worse, because now no one is accepting responsibility for the recommendation:

> The opening of a new office in Dayton is recommended.

Using the personal pronoun *you* in instructions clarifies the actor and personalizes the instructions, as in this passage from Internal Revenue Service (IRS) tax instructions:

> You can deduct the actual cost of running your car or truck or take the standard mileage rate. You must use actual costs if you do not own the vehicle or if you used more than one vehicle simultaneously (such as in fleet operations).

Take away the use of *you*, and the result would likely be the impersonal passive voice, harder to read and understand and vague about who is doing what:

> The actual cost of running a car or truck can be deducted or the standard mileage rate can be used. Actual costs must be used if the vehicle is not owned or if more than one vehicle is used simultaneously (such as in fleet operations).

In tax instructions, the IRS refers to itself as *we,* as in:

> If you want, we will figure the tax for you.

The use of *we* in instructions is appropriate, as long as it is clear who *we* is. In the previous example, the use of *IRS* would have worked about as well as *we.* But *we* sounds much more friendly and personal, which may have a positive effect on the audience.

Often, you would be wise to make clear the *references* of your terms at the beginning of your instructions. For example, at the beginning of an insurance policy, you might note that *we* refers to the insurance company and *you* refers to the policy holder.

Use Action Verbs

Using action verbs is closely related to using active voice and personal pronouns. All these style decisions help you avoid using *nominalizations,* which are nouns derived from verbs. For example, *instruction* comes from *instruct,* and *assessment* comes from *assess.*

There is nothing wrong with using nominalizations, as long as they are used properly. Using *instructions* in a sentence like this is fine, for example:

> Computer companies have learned that good instructions sell computers.

But you would be on soft ground and sinking fast if you wrote this passage in a letter to an office manager:

> Misuse of the computer network by your secretaries has become evident. Please make provision for your secretaries to receive proper instruction in the use of the network.

This passage is stuffy, wordy, and not specific. This rewrite is better:

> Your secretaries are misusing the computer network with personal mail. Please instruct them to use the network for business mail only.

In the revised passage, the writer uses action verbs and specifies what the problem actually is.

Unfortunately, you will find a good many nominalizations in technical writing, such as this one:

> The emission of sulfur dioxide from the factory is much greater than the emission of hydrogen sulfide.

If you find such a clumsy sentence in your work, think about where the action is and rewrite the sentence with an action verb:

> The factory emits much more sulfur dioxide than hydrogen sulfide.

When you are revising your work, look out for nominalizations. Better still, use the "find" or "search" function of your computer. Look for words that end in *-ment, -ion, -ance, -ence, -al,* and *-ing.* If you find any nominalizations, check to see if you have used them properly. If you have not, revise them by using action verbs.

Don't Introduce Unnecessary Complication

Both research and intuition will tell you that the more highly educated readers are, the more sentence complexity they can tolerate. But *no* readers appreciate sentences that are too long or tortured out of shape.

Think Subject-Verb

The subject and verb of a sentence are its frame, upon which you can hang various grammatical segments to expand or clarify the information provided by the subject and verb. To illustrate this process, here are a few examples:

> OPEC could easily produce half of all the oil consumed in the world.

By 2010, OPEC could easily produce half of all the oil produced in the world.

Because OPEC members control such a huge share of the world's high-quality, low-cost oil reserves, by 2010, OPEC could easily produce half of all the oil produced in the world.

None of these sentences should cause difficulty for a reader with at least high school reading ability. In all of them, the basic subject-verb frame stays clearly in view. The added grammatical segments provide additional information but do not excessively complicate matters.

Use a Reasonable Sentence Length

What is a *reasonable* sentence length? The answer to this question obviously relates closely to the abilities of your readers. Most high school graduates can read longer sentences that elementary schoolchildren, and most college-educated readers can read longer sentences than high school students. Moreover, readers familiar with the subject under discussion can read longer sentences than readers who are not.

As shown by the examples in the last section, sentences grow in length as information is added to them. At some point, they can be too long and too complicated, regardless of readers' abilities. The sentence in this example is probably too long for most readers:

Because of OPEC members', especially the Persian Gulf members', control over such a huge share of the world's high-quality, low-cost oil reserves, the willingness and ability of OPEC members to expand production capacity, including production potential from Kuwait and Iraq, and the limited ability of non-OPEC producers to expand production facilities, by 2010, OPEC could easily produce half of all the oil produced in the world, which will greatly influence prospects for world oil prices.

A reader's ability to handle long, complicated sentences relates not only to the reader's own skill but also to the skill with which the writer constructs sentences. Therefore, it is risky to set limits on sentence length. It seems clear, however, that sentences that exceed 40 or 50 words are too difficult for most people. Professional writers average about 20 words a sentence. That average is likely one that most writers should strive for.

Write Positively

Too many negative words in a sentence can cause unnecessary complication, particularly in instructions. The problem occurs when negative words—such as *no, none,* and *not*—are combined with words that begin with negative prefixes—such as *ir-* (*irrelevant*), *non-* (*noncommittal*), and *un-* (*unbroken*). For example, the first sentence that follows is more difficult to read than the second:

> The virus protection is not installed properly until the virus protection icon appears at the bottom of your screen.

> The virus protection is installed properly when the virus protection icon appears at the bottom of your screen.

In reading the first sentence, readers will have a momentary pause while translating the negative combination *not . . . until* into a positive statement. The second sentence, already written positively, presents no such complication.

Avoid Long Noun Strings

Using nouns to modify other nouns is commonplace in English. Expressions like *mail carrier* and *consumption level* are grammatically correct and understandable. But using long noun strings to modify other nouns introduces complications that raise difficulties for the reader, as in this example:

> Surplus production energy capacity price fluctuation control policies seem doomed to failure.

Policies is the word modified by the long noun string. That much is clear, but little else is. In the seven-word modifying phrase, the reader has to pause and sort out which words or groups of words modify other words or groups of words. The writer should do the sorting, perhaps in this way:

> The policies for controlling price fluctuations caused by surplus production in energy capacity seem doomed to failure.

Review your own writing to identify noun strings. Be wary if you see that you have put together more than three nouns to modify another noun without using clarifying hyphens or prepositions. You probably need to rewrite the sentence.

Check for Parallelism

Write parallel ideas in parallel grammatical form. In this well-written sentence, the writer uses parallelism to good effect:

> Storms, floods, droughts, and fires that accompanied the unusually strong El Niño of 1997–1998 took more than 30,000 lives, displaced about a third of a billion people, and in less than a year ran up tab of nearly 100 billion dollars in material damages.[4]

The three parallel verbs—*took, displaced,* and *ran up*—tie together the clauses of a fairly long sentence, making it easy to read despite its length.

In the next example, the writer starts the list of symptoms with two noun phrases, switches to an infinitive phrase, and ends with a dependent clause:

> Signs of a heart attack include a sensation of fullness, pain in the center of the chest, to faint, and when you feel a shortness of breath.

You really don't have to know all that grammatical terminology to recognize that this sentence has gone wrong somehow. It has become complicated and more difficult to understand than it should be. Fix the sentence by putting all the symptoms in the same grammatical form:

> Signs of a heart attack are a sensation of fullness, pain in the center of the chest, fainting, and shortness of breath.

When making a list, take care to keep all the elements of the list in parallel grammatical form, as the writer does in this example:

> Short-term climate anomalies, such as we experienced with El Niño, can serve as analogs for what might happen in the course of future global greenhouse warming. Some of the relevant impacts of the 1997–98 El Niño are listed below:
>
> - A rise of about six inches in sea level along the coast of California.
>
> - Substantially higher than normal temperatures over land.
>
> - Changes in precipitation patterns, leading to flooding in some areas (such as Chile, Peru, California, and the southeastern U.S.).[5]

The writer kept his list parallel by using noun phrases based on *rise,* *temperatures,* and *changes.* Also, the use of bullets (•) helps clarify and organize the list for readers.

5

Use Good
Page Design

Well-designed pages increase the accessibility of your report by helping readers see its organization. By making your presentation visually attractive, good design increases the likelihood that your audience will read carefully.

Important elements of good design are headings, headers and footers, appropriate type size and typeface, lists and informal tables, discreet typographical emphasis, and the ample use of white space.

Provide Headings

The use of headings lowers the density of type on the page and provides easy transitions from one topic to the next. Mainly, headings make information more accessible to readers.

Different levels of headings identify topics and subtopics within a document, making its organization clear to readers. By scanning headings or using them in conjunction with a matching table of contents (see pp. 84–85), readers can find the sections in documents they need or want to read. For example, an accountant reading a report about a new financial spreadsheet may be most interested in the how-to instructions. The accountant's boss, however, may be most interested in how the new spreadsheet may make the accountant more efficient.

Compare Figures 5.1 and 5.2 to see what a difference in readability a few well-placed headings can make.

At present, USGS investigates three types of severe coastal storm impacts: hurricanes in the southeast U.S., extra-tropical storm impacts on the U.S. west coast during El-Niño, and 'northeaster' impacts on the U.S. east coast.

Hurricanes are tropical storms that have a sustained wind speed greater than 75MPH. In the northern hemisphere, these low pressure systems rotate counterclockwise. As a hurricane approaches the coast, the wind speed on the right side of the storm is added to the forward speed of the storm. Hence, the greatest impacts from storm surge, wave battering and wind speed tend to occur to the right of the eye at landfall. Storm surge is an increase in sea level along the coast caused primarily by strong onshore winds and low barometric pressure. The strongest hurricanes are Category 5, having sustained wind speeds in excess of 155MPH and storm surge in excess of 6 m (20 ft). In recorded history, only two Category 5 hurricanes have made landfall in the United States.

During severe El-Niño, the jet stream over the Pacific Ocean tends to be more southerly than normal, guiding winter extra-tropical storms into California and bringing extensive rainfall and large waves to the California coast. During the severe El-Niños of 1982-83 and 1997-98 extensive coastal erosion and damage occurred along the west coast. Under El-Niño conditions of equatorial warming in the Pacific, hurricanes are less frequent in the north Atlantic. The reoccurrence of La-Niña, equatorial cooling in the Pacific, coincides with active hurricane seasons for the southeast United States.

Northeasters, or winter extra-tropical storms impacting the east coast of the United States, can cause considerable coastal change and damage. For example, one of the most destructive storms to ever impact the mid-Atlantic states was the Ash Wednesday storm of 1962. Extensive coastal change occurred over 1,000 km of coast. Northeasters owe their destructive power to their long duration. Winds are typically below hurricane force, but can persist for several days to a week generating large waves and enhanced storm surge. In comparison, hurricanes are more severe in terms of wind speed and storm surge but the shoreline impacts tend to be more localized, confined to order 100 km of coast. Hurricanes also tend to be more short-lived moving across coastal areas in hours rather than days.

FIGURE 5.1 Document without Headings

Source: Adapted from U.S. Geological Survey, *Hurricanes and Extreme Storm Impact Studies.* http://coastal.er.usgs.gov/hurricanes/storms.html#elnino (10 January 2000).

Hurricane and Extreme Storm Impact Studies
Hurricanes, El-Niño, & Northeasters—An Introduction

At present, USGS investigates three types of severe coastal storm impacts: hurricanes in the southeast U.S., extra-tropical storm impacts on the U.S. west coast during El-Niño, and 'northeaster' impacts on the U.S. east coast.

HURRICANES

Hurricanes are tropical storms that have a sustained wind speed greater than 75MPH. In the northern hemisphere, these low pressure systems rotate counterclockwise. As a hurricane approaches the coast, the wind speed on the right side of the storm is added to the forward speed of the storm. Hence, the greatest impacts from storm surge, wave battering and wind speed tend to occur to the right of the eye at landfall. Storm surge is an increase in sea level along the coast caused primarily by strong onshore winds and low barometric pressure. The strongest hurricanes are Category 5, having sustained wind speeds in excess of 155MPH and storm surge in excess of 6 m (20 ft). In recorded history, only two Category 5 hurricanes have made landfall in the United States.

EL-NIÑO

During severe El-Niño, the jet stream over the Pacific Ocean tends to be more southerly than normal, guiding winter extra-tropical storms into California and bringing extensive rainfall and large waves to the California coast. During the severe El-Niños of 1982-83 and 1997-98 extensive coastal erosion and damage occurred along the west coast. Under El-Niño conditions of equatorial warming in the Pacific, hurricanes are less frequent in the north Atlantic. The reoccurrence of La-Niña, equatorial cooling in the Pacific, coincides with active hurricane seasons for the southeast United States.

NORTHEASTERS

Northeasters, or winter extra-tropical storms impacting the east coast of the United States, can cause considerable coastal change and damage. For example, one of the most destructive storms to ever impact the mid-Atlantic states was the Ash Wednesday storm of 1962. Extensive coastal change occurred over 1,000 km of coast. Northeasters owe their destructive power to their long duration. Winds are typically below hurricane force, but can persist for several days to a week generating large waves and enhanced storm surge. In comparison, hurricanes are more severe in terms of wind speed and storm surge but the shoreline impacts tend to be more localized, confined to order 100 km of coast. Hurricanes also tend to be more short-lived moving across coastal areas in hours rather than days.

FIGURE 5.2   Document with Headings

Source: Adapted from U.S. Geological Survey, *Hurricanes and Extreme Storm Impact Studies.* http://coastal.er.usgs.gov/hurricanes/storms.html#elnino (10 January 2000).

Because the main role of headings is to increase accessibility, do not use more than three or four levels of headings. Too many headings chop a document into too many pieces and decrease, rather than increase, accessibility.

You will likely have two basic questions in using headings: (1) How do I phrase headings? and (2) How do I make headings noticeable and distinctive?

Phrasing Headings

Headings can be questions, short sentences, single words, or phrases of various types. For example, a document about government benefits might contain a section on qualifying for those benefits. The heading for this section could be phrased in various ways:

Who Can Qualify?

You May Qualify

Qualifications

Qualifying for Benefits

Questions seem to work well for headings, perhaps because they mirror what is in readers' minds. But the really important principle is that each heading should accurately identify what the section contains. For that reason, most headings should be substantive, rather than generic. A *generic* heading is a heading like "Part One," with no further identification. A generic heading such as "Introduction" or "Conclusion" serves the purpose adequately, but when used elsewhere in reports, generic headings do not give readers enough information. In the body of a report, use *substantive* headings that tell readers what they can expect to find in the sections, like these:

Biofilm Formation

Trends in Computer Use

Dangers in Self-Medication

Headings within any section of a document must be grammatically parallel (see pp. 33–34). For example, all the major topic headings must be parallel. The subtopic headings within a major section must also be parallel, but they do not have to be parallel to subtopic headings in other major sections. The Table of Contents for the two parts of this book makes this concept clear:

Part One	**The Seven Principles of Technical Writing**
1	Know Your Purpose
2	Know Your Audience
3	Choose and Organize Your Content around Your Purpose and Audience
4	Write Clearly and Precisely
5	Use Good Page Design
6	Think Visually
7	Write Ethically
Part Two	**The Formats of Technical Writing**
8	Elements of Reports
9	Formats of Reports
10	Formats of Correspondence

The headings for the two parts are parallel noun phrases. (They are also substantive.) The chapter headings in Part One are all active/imperative sentences. The headings in Part Two are all noun phrases: parallel with each other but not with the headings in Part One.

Making Headings Noticeable and Distinctive

Good choices of words and grammatical forms help make headings noticeable and distinctive. Beyond that, good choices of typographical formats for your headings make them noticeable and distinguish different levels of headings.

Figures 5.3 and 5.4 show some of the various types of headings available to you. Notice that distinctiveness is obtained through such devices as underlining, spacing, italicizing, capitalizing, centering, indenting, using different type sizes, and so forth. However, all these headings are in the same typeface. Using different typefaces for different headings can lead to a gimmicky overkill.

Choose three or four of the available styles and stick with them through your document. Keep each heading with the section of text it identifies. Don't leave a heading dangling at the bottom of a page and start the section it identifies on the next page. Include at least two lines of the section with the heading. If you can't, move everything to the next page.

WRITE CLEARLY AND PRECISELY

USE GOOD PAGE DESIGN

<u>Write Clearly and Precisely</u>

   <u>Use Good Page Design</u>

   <u>Write clearly and precisely</u>.

Use Good Page Design

Write Clearly and Precisely

Use Good Page Design

   Write Clearly and Precisely

   Use good page design.

FIGURE 5.3   Examples of Heading Styles

FRANCE

GEOGRAPHY
France is located ▓▓▓▓▓▓▓▓▓▓▓▓▓▓▓▓▓▓▓▓
▓▓▓▓▓▓▓▓▓▓▓▓▓▓▓▓▓▓▓▓▓▓▓▓▓

Boundaries
Bounded on the west by ▓▓▓▓▓▓▓▓▓▓▓▓▓▓
▓▓▓▓▓▓▓▓▓▓▓▓▓▓▓▓▓▓▓▓▓▓▓▓▓

Land Use
Although mostly flat plains ▓▓▓▓▓▓▓▓▓▓
▓▓▓▓▓▓▓▓▓▓▓▓▓▓▓▓▓▓▓▓▓▓▓▓▓

    Arable land. About 33 percent of ▓▓▓▓▓▓
▓▓▓▓▓▓▓▓▓▓▓▓▓▓▓▓▓▓▓▓▓▓▓▓▓

    Forest and woodland. About 27 percent of ▓▓▓
▓▓▓▓▓▓▓▓▓▓▓▓▓▓▓▓▓▓▓▓▓▓▓▓▓

POPULATION
The age structure of ▓▓▓▓▓▓▓▓▓▓▓▓▓▓▓▓
▓▓▓▓▓▓▓▓▓▓▓▓▓▓▓▓▓▓▓▓▓▓▓▓▓

GOVERNMENT
The French government is ▓▓▓▓▓▓▓▓▓▓▓▓▓
▓▓▓▓▓▓▓▓▓▓▓▓▓▓▓▓▓▓▓▓▓▓▓▓▓

FIGURE 5.4   Examples of Headings in Document

Use Headers and Footers

Headers and footers are other ways of keeping readers on track. A *header* is a phrase that identifies the document or perhaps a section of it. As the name implies, a header appears at the head, or top, of the page. A *footer* contains the same basic information but appears at the foot, or bottom, of the page.

In a short document, the title of the piece is usually presented in a header or footer. Sometimes, a header or footer may include the date and the name of the author of the document. In a longer document divided into chapters or major sections, the chapter or section heading is usually presented in a header or footer. Note that in this book, the part title is indicated on each left-hand page and the chapter title is indicated on each right-hand page.

Page numbers may appear with headers or footers or separately. Often, the information identifying the document or section will be in a header and the page number will be in a footer. Do not put an identifying header or footer on the title page or on the first pages of major sections, such as chapters. Do put page numbers on every page except the title page, however.

See Figure 5.5 for a selection of typical headers and footers.

Choose an Appropriate Type Size and Typeface

Deciding what is an *appropriate* type size and typeface most often means choosing type that eases the reader's task.

Type Size

Type sizes are expressed in units called *points*. The higher the number, or *point size,* the bigger the type:

9-point type

10-point type

12-point type

14-point type

18-point type

24-point type

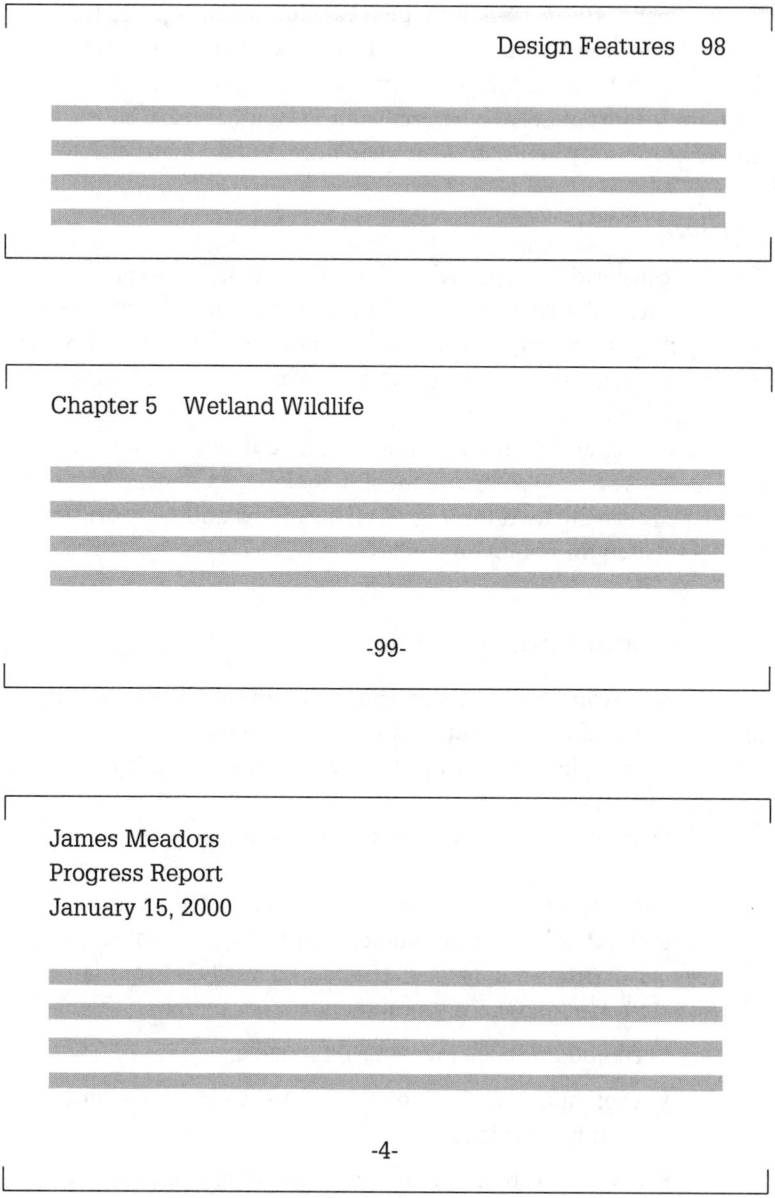

Design Features 98

Chapter 5 Wetland Wildlife

-99-

James Meadors
Progress Report
January 15, 2000

-4-

FIGURE 5.5 Typical Headers and Footers

In general, 10- to 12-point type is easy for most people to read. Use these sizes for the text in reports and correspondence. You may choose slightly larger type, such as 14-point, for headings to make them stand out from the text. Reserve type sizes from 18-point and up for brochures and other specialty items, for which you may want dramatic effects.

Typeface

The two categories of type are serif and sans serif. *Serif* type has small extenders (called *serifs*) coming off the letters, as in the type used for most of the text in this book, which is Minion. Sans serif type does not have these extenders, as in Helvetica type, which is used for some of the tables and figures in this book.

Conventional design wisdom says that serif type is easier to read and that sans serif type is more modern looking. As done in this book, serif type is usually used for large sections of text and sans serif type is frequently used for graphs and tables.

Use Lists and Informal Tables

You can save words and open up your text by using lists and informal tables. Separate these elements from your text by indenting them at the left or both margins. Do not identify lists or informal tables with titles or table numbers.

A list with its accompanying text looks like this:

Steps to stop Listeria . . . *Listeria* is a common food-borne bacterium that can cause symptoms including nausea, vomiting, cramps, diarrhea and fever. To protect yourself and your family from *Listeria*, take these precautions:

- Thoroughly cook raw animal products.

- Thoroughly wash all food that is to be eaten raw, such as fruits and vegetables.

- Keep foods to be eaten raw separate from uncoooked meats.

- Wash hands, knives and cutting boards with hot soapy water.

> In addition, those most vulnerable to *Listeria* infections,
> such as pregnant women, the elderly, and those with weakened
> immune systems, also should . . .[1]

Notice how bullets (•) are used to identify the list items. Numbers may also be used but only if the order of the items in the list is important.

An informal table is essentially a list that contains columns (see Figure 5.6). Present informal tables as you do lists, but take care to align the separate columns of information. (See Chapter 6 for a discussion of formal tables.)

Use Emphasis Carefully

Use typographical variations to emphasize important points in your reports or correspondence. Variations include the following:

boldface

<u>underlining</u>

italic

larger type size

ALL CAPITAL LETTERS

These five states have the largest projected net increases in immigrants, 1995 to 2025 (in millions):

California	8.8
New York	3.9
Florida	1.9
New Jersey	1.2
Illinois	1.0

States with lower projected increases ▬▬▬▬▬▬▬
▬▬▬▬▬▬▬▬▬▬▬▬▬

FIGURE 5.6   An Informal Table

When using any of these means of emphasis, be careful not to overdo it. A page with too many things emphasized will look cluttered, and the emphasis will be lost. Be particularly careful not to use all capital letters for more than one line. Because we rely on the ups and downs of capitals and lowercase letters in our reading, using all capitals raises the difficulty of reading. See Figure 5.7 for an example of typographical emphasis.

Leave Ample White Space

For ease of reading, a printed page should be about 50 percent type and 50 percent *white space* (a design term for "empty space"). Headings, lists, informal tables, and paragraphing all contribute to white space. In addition, you gain more white space with adequate margins, medium-length lines, and proper spacing. All measurements given here are based on using a standard 8-1/2″ x 11″ page.

Margins

Leave 1″ for the top and side margins and 1-1/2″ for the bottom margin. If you intend to bind your document, leave 1-1/2″ to 2″ on the side to be bound (usually the left).

Medium-Length Lines

Line length depends somewhat on the size and face of type used, but in most cases, a line of 50 to 70 characters (which is about 10 to 12 words) will be about right. In a double-column format, about 35 characters (or 5 words) per line is appropriate.

Should you *justify* your lines or not? That is, should your lines be even at both the left and right margins? Many word processors, in an attempt to justify the right margin, leave unattractive "rivers" of white space running through the text. Given this problem, you are better off in most instances to leave the right margin *ragged*—that is, unjustified. In any case, there seems to be little difference in readability between justified pages and ragged-right pages.

Global Enterprises

DATE	15 September 2000
TO	Roy Goss
	Ann Manchester
	Jim Morris
	Brittany Osborn
	Al Smith
FROM	Pat Macintosh
SUBJECT	Schedule for Reporting Monthly Design Meetings

Thank you all for agreeing to report our monthly meetings. What follows is the schedule for the year:

2000

October	Pat Macintosh
November	Jim Morris
December	Brittany Osborn

2001

January	Roy Goss
February	Ann Manchester
March	Al Smith
April	Pat Macintosh
May	Jim Morris
June	Brittany Osborn
July	Roy Goss
August	Ann Manchester
September	Al Smith

If you can't report the month for which you are scheduled, call me and I'll arrange a switch. If I'm not available, call one of the other reporters listed to take your place.

Please use a memo format for your reports. Address them to Dave Buehler, and send copies to Sally Barker and me.

FIGURE 5.7   Example of Typographical Emphasis within Memo

Proper Spacing

You have the choices of single-space, space-and-a-half, and double-space. Lines in memos and letters are traditionally single-spaced, with double-spacing between paragraphs. To achieve more white space in other documents, use space-and-a-half or double-spacing. Double-space the first draft of any document to allow room for corrections, changes, and scribbling.

6

Think Visually

As you think about and plan your documents, think visually as well as verbally. Graphics of various kinds play a major role in technical writing, often presenting data and ideas more efficiently and precisely than words. In technical writing, you will use graphics to show objects, processes, and data. As you look at each sample graphic in this chapter, notice that the caption may be placed at either the bottom or top. Sometimes, the stylesheets for certain publications will dictate the placement of graphic captions. At other times, it will be your decision. In any case, be consistent with your placement throughout a document.

Showing Objects

The word *object* covers a lot of territory. It can mean a machine, mountain, tool, animal, pond, glacier, the inner ear—indeed, any material thing that you can see or feel. Photographs and drawings are used to portray objects.

Figure 1—*The factory duster with a flange added to elevate outlet airflow to 60°. **A** = elevation flange, **B** = chemical hopper, **C** = air intake, **D** = adjustable baffle plate in air outlet.*

FIGURE 6.1   Photograph of Mechanism. The annotations below the photograph identify the labeled parts of the mechanism.

Source: D. L. Copes, D. O'Rourke, and W. K. Randall, "Field Testing a Modified Duster for Supplemental Mass Pollination in Douglas-Fir Seed Orchards," *Tree Planters' Notes* 46 (1995): 120.

Photographs

Photographs have the advantage of realism. As part of a mechanism description, photographs help readers see the mechanism as it really is. Figure 6.1 shows how words and an annotated photo work together for better understanding. As illustrated in this figure, annotations are typically written horizontally for ease of reading.

The photograph in Figure 6.2 shows the size of a deer tick nymph through comparison with a thumb. Such things as coins and actual rulers included in photographs can also efficiently show scale.

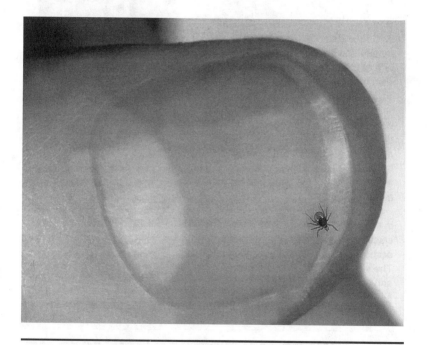

FIGURE 6.2　Photograph Showing Size of Deer Tick Nymph. The size of the tick compared to that of a human thumb gives a good idea of scale.

Source: Carol Lewis, "New Vaccine Targets Lyme Disease," *FDA Consumer* May–June 1999: 13.

The Collapse of the Interstate-5/ State Highway-14 Interchange

The collapsed I-5/SH-14 interchange (see cover) was one of the most spectacular and costliest damage sites resulting from the earthquake. To determine what happened at the site, USGS scientists deployed instruments on the standing sections of the interchange bridges and on the surrounding ground at the bases of the pier supports. The instruments were used to obtain aftershock records for (1) determining the dominant vibrational modes in which the bridges responded to shaking, and (2) estimating the main-shock motions responsible for the collapse.

Using accelerations and velocities from the four largest aftershocks, USGS engineers calculated ground-to-deck *transfer functions*. The functions defined the transfer of vibration from the ground to the bridge deck in the horizontal and vertical directions, and longitudinally along the bridge spans. Different methods for calculating the functions gave consistent estimates of dominant frequencies of the deck—0.4, 0.7, and 3.2 hertz in the horizontal, longitudinal, and vertical directions, respectively.

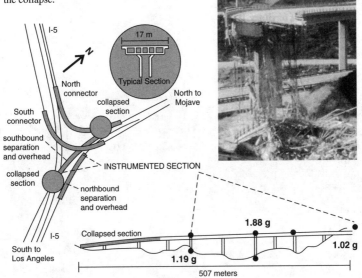

USGS engineers placed instruments throughout a section of the freeway bridge adjacent to the section that collapsed during the earthquake. Using aftershock recordings and data from nearby stations that recorded the main shock, they were able to relate the collapse to accelerations that greatly exceeded those for which the bridge was designed. Accelerations calculated for the base of the bridge (1.19g and 1.02g) translated into an acceleration of 1.88g on the deck. The 1.88g value represents conditions of the failed structure, and not those of the original continuous structure.

FIGURE 6.3   Photograph of Collapsed Freeway Span with Accompanying Text and Diagrams

Source: U.S. Geological Survey, *USGS Response to an Urban Earthquake Northridge '94,* Open File Report 92-263 (1996): 52. http://geohazards.cr.usgs.gov/northridge/ (10 January 2000).

The photograph in Figure 6.3 of a collapsed freeway span adds both drama and realism to the accompanying text and diagrams. Unless they are very carefully made, photographs have the disadvantage of including extraneous detail, as is obvious in Figure 6.1. The mushrooms in Figure 6.4 have been more carefully photographed, such that extraneous detail has been held to a minimum.

FIGURE 6.4   Photograph of Mushrooms. Careful photography will minimize background detail.

Source: Marian Segal, "Stalking the Wild Mushroom," *FDA Consumer* October 1994: 23.

Drawings

Drawings give you the advantage of control. You can eliminate extraneous detail and easily emphasize whatever you want to emphasize. You can do cutaways of objects that would be difficult or impossible to show in a photograph. Drawings also can be easily annotated. All these advantages are apparent in Figures 6.5 and 6.6.

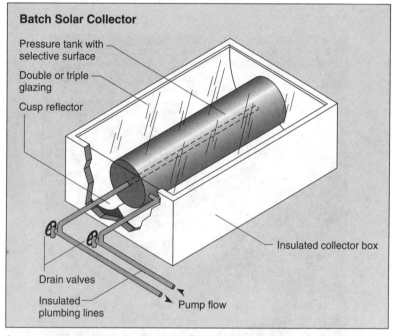

Batch Solar Collector

Pressure tank with selective surface

Double or triple glazing

Cusp reflector

Insulated collector box

Drain valves

Insulated plumbing lines

Pump flow

An open-loop system heats household water directly in the collectors. One such type of open-loop system is the batch heater. This system is simply a black tank filled with water and placed inside a south-facing, insulated, glazed box, where it absorbs solar energy.

FIGURE 6.5   Drawing of Batch Solar Collector

Source: U.S. Department of Energy, *Solar Water Heating* (Washington, DC: Information Services Program, 1996) 4.

Components of a Typical*
Residential Heating and
Cooling System

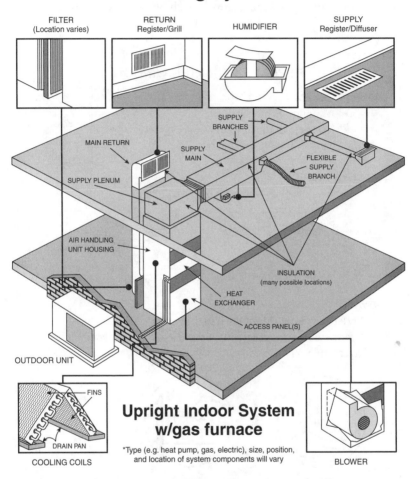

FILTER
(Location varies)

RETURN
Register/Grill

HUMIDIFIER

SUPPLY
Register/Diffuser

SUPPLY
BRANCHES

MAIN RETURN

SUPPLY
MAIN

FLEXIBLE
SUPPLY
BRANCH

SUPPLY PLENUM

AIR HANDLING
UNIT HOUSING

INSULATION
(many possible locations)

HEAT
EXCHANGER

ACCESS PANEL(S)

OUTDOOR UNIT

FINS

Upright Indoor System
w/gas furnace

DRAIN PAN

COOLING COILS

*Type (e.g. heat pump, gas, electric), size, position,
and location of system components will vary

BLOWER

FIGURE 6.6   Drawing of Residential Heating and Cooling System

Source: U.S. Environmental Protection Agency, *Should You Have the Air Ducts in Your
Home Cleaned?* (Washington, DC: GPO, 1997) 5.

Showing Processes

Describing processes is a major activity in technical writing (see pp. 105–12). Many process descriptions benefit from the descriptive power of accompanying graphics. Figure 6.7 shows how a combination of

---

REPLACE A BROKEN WINDOW

YOUR PROBLEM
- A window is broken.
- Heat is lost around window panes where putty is missing or dried out.

WHAT YOU NEED
- Window glass—correct size
- Putty or glazing compound
- Putty knife
- Hammer
- Pliers
- Glazier points

HOW-TO
1. Work from the outside of the frame. (Fig. 1)
2. Remove the broken glass with pliers to avoid cutting your fingers. (Fig. 2)

Fig. 1   Fig. 2

FIGURE 6.7   Words and Illustrations Working Together to Show Process.
The simple but excellent page design—using headings, bullets, and numbers—makes for easy reading.

Source: U.S. Department of Agriculture, *Simple Home Repairs: Inside* (Washington, DC: U.S. Government Printing Office, 1986) 11–12.

words and illustrations work together to instruct a reader how to accomplish a technical process.

Figures 6.8 and 6.9 illustrate *flowcharts*—graphs that are specifically designed to illustrate processes. Flowcharts are suitable for all levels of readers.

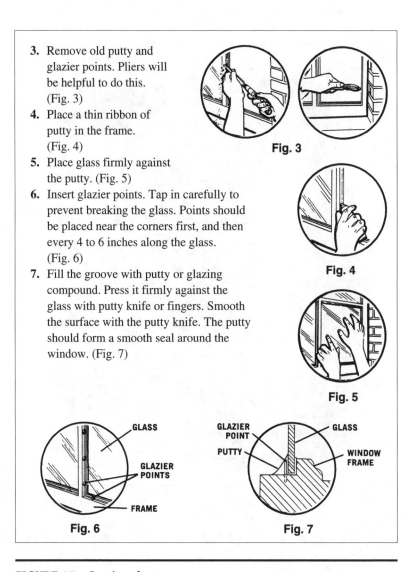

3. Remove old putty and glazier points. Pliers will be helpful to do this. (Fig. 3)
4. Place a thin ribbon of putty in the frame. (Fig. 4)
5. Place glass firmly against the putty. (Fig. 5)
6. Insert glazier points. Tap in carefully to prevent breaking the glass. Points should be placed near the corners first, and then every 4 to 6 inches along the glass. (Fig. 6)
7. Fill the groove with putty or glazing compound. Press it firmly against the glass with putty knife or fingers. Smooth the surface with the putty knife. The putty should form a smooth seal around the window. (Fig. 7)

Fig. 3

Fig. 4

Fig. 5

GLASS

GLAZIER POINTS

FRAME

Fig. 6

GLAZIER POINT

PUTTY

GLASS

WINDOW FRAME

Fig. 7

FIGURE 6.7 Continued

Processing of Milk Treated with rbST

Milk from rbST-treated and untreated cows is collected in the same manner. Milk from each farm is tested for antibiotic drug residues. If there are unsafe drug residues, the entire tanker of milk is dumped. If no residues are found the tanker delivers the milk to the processor who readies it for market. Antibiotics are used to treat mastitis, an inflammation of the cow's udder, which is more common in rbST-treated cows.

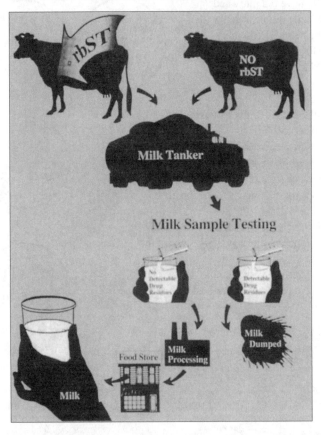

FIGURE 6.8   Flowchart. Flowcharts can be used to show decision points in a process, as demonstrated by this chart.

Source: Kevin L. Ropp, "New Animal Drug Increases Milk Production," *FDA Consumer* May 1994: 26.

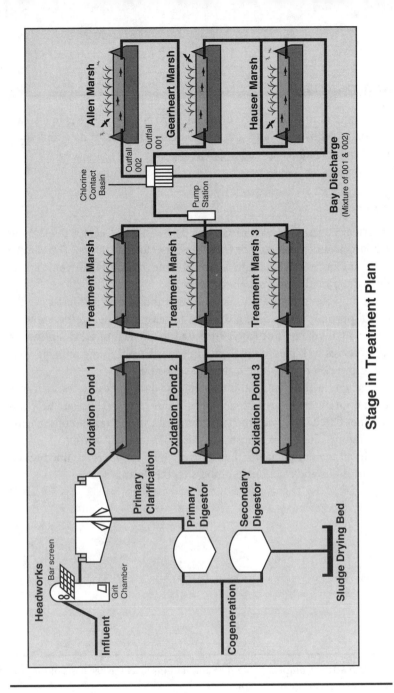

FIGURE 6.9 Flowchart Showing Wastewater Treatment Plan

Source: U.S. Environmental Protection Agency, *Constructed Wetlands for Wastewater Treatment and Wildlife Habitat* (Washington, DC: GPO, 1993) 62.

Showing Data

Tables and graphs of all sorts are great word and space savers in displaying data. With tables and graphs, you can summarize data and show trends and relationships among them.

Tables

Informal tables work well for simple data displays (see pp. 44–45). But for larger and more complex displays, use formal tables. The sample table in Figure 6.10 illustrates a formal table. Its accompanying annotations describe the table's main features.

The table in Figure 6.10 is complex enough that its lines serve the useful purpose of separating the data for easy reading. In less complex tables, many of the lines are eliminated (as in Figure 6.11), and white space serves to separate the data. Let ease of reading the table be your guide, but eliminate as much clutter as possible.

When need be, you can interpret your data in headnotes, captions, and annotations. Many of the figures in this chapter illustrate how this is done. Often, you will interpret your data in the text accompanying your figures. Figure 6.12 illustrates this table-text relationship

In all the sample tables, notice that whole numbers are lined up on the last digits and fractional numbers on the decimals.

FIGURE 6.10   Complex Table. The annotations label the key parts of the   ▶
table and describe their functions.

Source: U.S. Department of Commerce, *Statistical Abstract of the United States,* 118th ed. (Washington, DC: GPO, 1998) 616.

Table number and title → **No. 1001. Civilian Employment of Scientists, Engineers, and Technicians, by Occupation and Industry: 1996**

Unit indicator → Explanatory headnote → [In thousands. Based on sample and subject to sampling error. For details, see source]

Column heads and subheads

OCCUPATION	Total[1]	Mining[2]	Construction	Manufacturing	Transportation[3]	Trade	FIRE[4]	Services	Government	Self-employed
				WAGE AND SALARY WORKERS						
Scientists, engineers, and technicians	4,885.5	54.6	67.2	1,394.5	208.9	236.5	192.1	1,792.2	694.2	235.9
Scientists	665.7	11.4	0.4	79.9	5.4	3.8	11.8	258.9	197.9	92.5
Physical scientists	206.7	9.9	0.4	51.3	3.0	2.4	0.8	81.6	47.2	10.2
Life scientists	180.0	0.2	0.1	27.1	1.2	1.4	0.4	62.9	74.7	8.3
Mathematical scientists	15.6	(NA)	(NA)	1.5	0.4	(NA)	3.1	4.5	4.8	1.3
Social scientists	263.5	1.3	(NA)	(NA)	0.8	(NA)	7.6	109.9	71.2	72.7
Computer systems analysts, engineers and scientists	932.8	3.7	2.1	196.6	42.2	60.8	86.5	375.0	107.4	58.4
Engineers[5]	1,382.4	18.9	31.0	620.4	68.7	39.1	10.5	370.0	177.9	45.8
Civil engineers	196.1	0.6	10.9	7.5	5.3	0.5	0.4	86.6	71.3	13.0
Electrical/electronics	367.2	0.6	9.4	163.6	34.6	13.5	1.3	96.1	34.9	13.1
Mechanical engineers	227.9	1.6	5.1	131.2	4.2	7.2	(NA)	61.6	11.8	4.0
Engineering and science technicians	1,235.8	15.7	29.4	432.8	66.9	91.7	4.3	423.0	154.9	11.8
Electrical/electronics technicians	297.4	1.0	7.9	104.3	21.4	69.5	1.4	70.0	20.3	1.7
Engineering technicians	400.2	4.9	4.2	150.9	25.5	11.4	0.3	105.9	92.9	3.2
Drafters	309.9	1.9	16.9	96.5	16.7	7.1	1.3	152.2	10.2	4.6
Science technicians	228.3	8.0	0.4	81.1	3.3	3.7	1.2	94.9	31.5	2.3
Surveyors	100.7	2.4	2.6	0.1	2.8	(NA)	0.7	62.5	22.0	7.5
Computer programmers	568.0	2.4	1.5	64.8	22.8	41.0	78.3	302.9	34.0	20.0

Stub heading → OCCUPATION

Notes —
NA Not available.   [1]Includes agriculture, forestry, and fishing not shown separately.   [2]Includes oil and gas extraction.
[3]Includes communications and public utilities.   [4]Finance, insurance, and real estate.   [5]Includes kinds of engineers and technicians not shown separately.

Source: U.S. Bureau of Labor Statistics, *Monthly Labor Review*, November 1997; and unpublished data. (Data collected biennially.)

61

Nursery production of tree planting stock by public,
industrial, and other private nurseries in FY 1997:

	Million seedlings	Percent of total
Nurseries		
Federal	53	3.3
State	348	21.4
Local government	5	0.3
Forest industry	852	52.5
Other industry	366	22.5
Total	1,624	100.0

FIGURE 6.11   Simple Table. Use no more lines in a table than are necessary to make data easily readable.

Source: Robert J. Moulton, "Tree Planting in the United States," *Tree Planters' Notes* 49 (1999): 10.

Graphs

Bar, pie, line, and map graphs are all commonly used in technical writing. Pictographs are sometimes used but mainly for nontechnical audiences. All graphs can be used to summarize and to show trends and relationships. Bar and pie graphs show well the relationships among data. They are good for all levels of audience, technical and nontechnical.

Line graphs are superior to bar graphs in showing the shapes of data. Are the numbers increasing? decreasing? forming a bell curve? Line graphs show these trends well, but be mindful of your audience. Line graphs work well for technical audiences, but unless the graphs are simple, nontechnical audiences may have trouble reading them. Consider using map graphs when there is a geographical component to your

Cuba's total labor force, estimated at 4.3 million in 1990, will grow to only 5.5 million by 2010, assuming there is no migration from the island. This 26-percent increase is far below the 67-percent growth projected for the region as a whole. It would be further reduced by emigration, the impact of which can be estimated by making assumptions about its size. If a constant total net emigration of 25,000 per year is assumed, the increase would be only 19 percent, to about 5.2 million (see Table 1, below).

Table 1: Projected Cuban Labor Force, All Ages (millions)

	No Net Emigration			Constant Net Emigration 25,000/Year		
	Male	Female	Total	Male	Female	Total
1990	2.9	1.4	4.3	2.9	1.4	4.3
1995	3.2	1.6	4.8	3.2	1.6	4.8
2000	3.4	1.8	5.2	3.3	1.7	5.0
2005	3.5	1.8	5.3	3.3	1.8	5.1
2010	3.6	1.9	5.5	3.3	1.8	5.2

The Age Divide

The more striking story appears when the labor force is divided by age into two groups: 15–39 and 40–64. The younger portion of the labor force will increase by less than 4 percent by 2010 under the no emigration assumption, and it would actually *decrease* by 3 percent under the constant migration scenario described above (see Table 2, below). The decline is even greater among males. The proportionate share of the younger labor force will slip from 66 percent to 54 percent, and the median age of the whole labor force—already the oldest in the region—will rise from 33.5 in 1990 to 38.9 by 2010.

Table 2: Projected Cuban Labor Force, Age 15–39 (millions) (assuming constant net emigration 25,000/year)

	Male	Female	Total*
1990	1.8	1.0	2.9
1995	2.0	1.1	3.1
2000	2.0	1.2	3.2
2005	1.9	1.2	3.0
2010	1.7	1.1	2.8

*May not equal sum of male and female components owing to rounding.

FIGURE 6.12   Two Tables with Accompanying Text. Tables display data well, but often, they must be explained and interpreted in accompanying text.

Source: Adapted from David G. Smith, "Cuba's Approaching Youth 'Bust,'" *Geographic and Global Issues* Spring 1994: 9–10.

data. As you do with tables, provide whatever interpretation is needed on the graph or in the accompanying text.

Figures 6.13 through 6.17 illustrate various kinds of graphs in use. Each figure caption points out the graph's features and principles of their use.

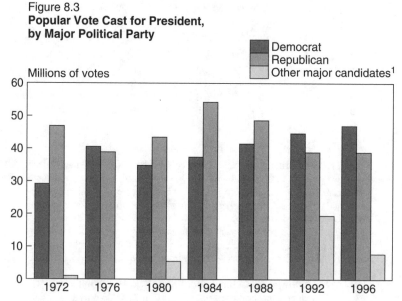

Figure 8.3
Popular Vote Cast for President, by Major Political Party

1 1972—American, John Schmitz; 1980—Independent, John Anderson; 1992—Independent, Ross Perot; 1996 Reform, Ross Perot.
Source: Chart prepared by U.S. Bureau of the Census. For data, see Tables 458 and 459.

FIGURE 6.13   Typical Bar Graph. When color is not used, use different degrees of shading to distinguish among bars. Cross-hatching is not a good choice because the moiré effect it produces can distract the reader. Avoid clutter of any kind. Do not use a complete grid unless reading the graph precisely is the reason for the graph. Notice that because the highest bar is in the 50 million range, the graph only goes to 60 million. Do not waste space in graphs.

Source: U.S. Department of Commerce, *Statistical Abstract of the United States,* 118th ed. (Washington DC: GPO, 1998) 278.

Principles of Tables and Graphs

Graphs and tables should be:

- Clear, uncluttered, and efficient
- Suited to their readers
- Interpreted as needed with notes, captions, annotations, lines, keys, arrows, and text (Footnotes are internal to tables and graphs and marked by numbers, letters, or symbols, such as asterisks[*].)
- Placed near their textual references
- Referred to when needed
- Numbered and have succinct titles: "Average Annual Pay, by State: 1999 and 2000" not "A Summary of Average Annual Pay, by State: 1999 and 2000"
- Well made and aesthetically pleasing but not artsy (Too much decoration gets in the way of the message.)
- Legible
- Honest and truthful (see pp. 72–76)

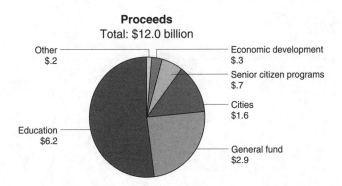

Proceeds
Total: $12.0 billion

Other $.2

Economic development $.3

Senior citizen programs $.7

Cities $1.6

Education $6.2

General fund $2.9

Source: Chart prepared by U.S. Bureau of the Census. For data, see Table 523.

FIGURE 6.14   Pie Graph. In constructing a pie graph, use a rational order for the slices, generally large to small or small to large. Keep the labels horizontal to the page. When there is room, you may label inside the slice, but keep the lettering horizontal.

Source: U.S. Department of Commerce, *Statistical Abstract of the United States*, 118th ed. (Washington DC: GPO, 1998) 306.

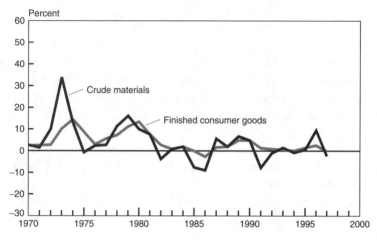

Figure 15.1
Annual Percentage Change in Producer Price Indexes by Stage of Processing: 1970 to 1997

Source: Chart prepared by U.S. Bureau of the Census. For data, see Table 777.

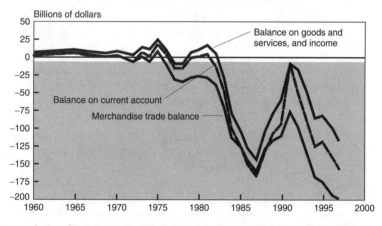

Figure 28.1
U.S. International Transaction Balances: 1960 to 1997

Source: Chart prepared by U.S. Bureau of the Census. For data, see Table 1302.

FIGURE 6.15 Two Typical Line Graphs. Each graph is labeled directly on the graph, using lettering horizontal to the page rather than using a key. Lines are kept distinct by using a mixture of dots, dashes, and shadings.

Source: U.S. Department of Commerce, *Statistical Abstract of the United States*, 118th ed. (Washington DC: GPO, 1998) 488, 782.

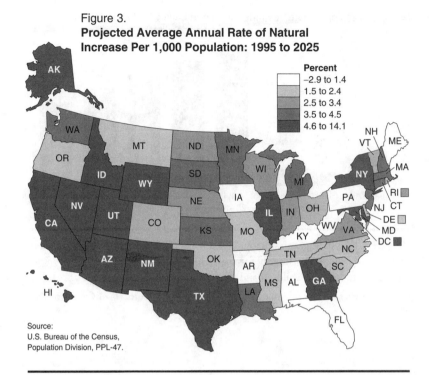

Figure 3.
Projected Average Annual Rate of Natural Increase Per 1,000 Population: 1995 to 2025

Percent
-2.9 to 1.4
1.5 to 2.4
2.5 to 3.4
3.5 to 4.5
4.6 to 14.1

Source:
U.S. Bureau of the Census,
Population Division, PPL-47.

FIGURE 6.16 Map Graph. Map graphs are very effective when geography is a factor, as it is in this graph that projects trends in state populations. Different degress of shading, not cross-hatching, distinguish the different percentage changes.

Source: Paul Campbell, *Current Population Reports* (Washington DC: U.S. Department of Commerce, 1997) 2.

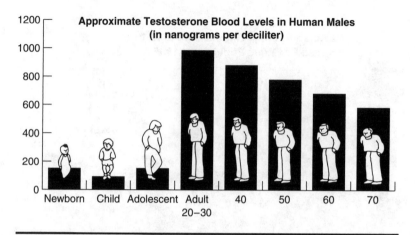

FIGURE 6.17 Pictograph. Pictographs are essentially bar graphs with human interest; they are used primarily for nontechnical audiences. Be sure the things depicted—in this case, children and men—can be easily recognized.

Source: Ken Flieger, "Testosterone: Key to Masculinity and More," *FDA Consumer* May 1995: 31.

7

Write Ethically

Ethical systems, whether religious or philosophical, agree that it is unethical to lie, cheat, and steal. Some systems grant a few exceptions, such as white social lies, a mother stealing for her starving child, and deceiving the enemy in time of war. But in general, the agreement is universal.

Morality consists of being ethical when it would be safer, more convenient, and more profitable to be unethical. Thus, morality does not always come easily. People are often tempted to commit unethical acts for personal gain, out of loyalty to organizations, or out of fear of the consequences they will face if seen as being disloyal—a "whistle blower," for example.

Technical writing has consequences. On the basis of feasibility studies and proposals, governments and businesses spend millions, even billions, of dollars. People follow instructions, expecting that their safety or the safety of their equipment will not be compromised by misstatements. Scientists base future research on past research reports. Researchers who misrepresent results or tell outright lies in their reports can mislead other scientists for years. Therefore, a moral imperative exists for technical and scientific writers to write ethically.

The principles that follow tell you how to prepare reports ethically. They cannot make you act morally. Only you can do that.[1]

Don't Hide or Suppress Unfavorable Data

Imagine that you are an engineer working as an inspector for a state environmental protection agency. You have just inspected the waste disposal facilities of a small city. You find that the city's effluent discharge into a nearby river does not meet state standards. You inform the city engineer, an old college buddy, of the situation. He informs you that the city is aware of the problem and is moving rapidly to solve it. He asks that you keep the effluent problem out of your report. Having the state come down on the city will just delay things, he says.

Should you suppress the information to honor an old friendship? The answer, according to the Engineering Ethics Board, is that you should not.[2] The board has decided in many similar cases that such behavior is unethical. Because public safety is paramount as part of an engineer's ethical code, it overrides not only friendship but even confidentiality agreements.

Similar situations may arise in writing proposals and research reports (see pp. 118–21 and 123–26). In a proposal, the temptation is to hide material that would indicate your company is not suited for the work it proposes to do. In a research report, the data might show that your theory is not as sound as you think. In both situations, the temptation is to hide or suppress the data.

Obviously, the people who read your reports, whatever kinds of reports they may be, put their implicit trust in your preparing honest, complete reports. To violate that trust would be to act immorally.

Don't Exaggerate Favorable Data

Exaggerating favorable data is the reverse of suppressing unfavorable data. In writing a proposal, you might exaggerate the experience of your company's scientists, making them sound more expert than they really are. In a feasibility report or the analysis section of a research report, to support the decision or conclusion you want, you might give favorable data more weight than they deserve.

Is any such exaggeration ever ethical? Where proposals and other sales documents are concerned, the expression "Put your best foot forward" applies. That is, it is legitimate in advertisements and proposals to show how your product or service meets the needs of potential customers. You may do so by emphasizing the strong points of your product or service. You are *expected* to do so by both your organization and your customer. But to be ethical, such emphasis must not overstep the bounds and distort the true facts. For example, in a proposal, you could legitimately emphasize the Ph.D. in chemical engineering held by your lead investigator, but it would be unethical to imply that her experience matched the needs of the client if, in fact, it did not.

In nonsales documents, such as research reports and feasibility reports, anything less than the relevant data, accompanied by an objective analysis, would be unethical.

Don't Make False Implications

In making a *false implication,* you are actually telling the truth but in a way that leads readers to the wrong conclusion. For example, imagine that you are writing a proposal for construction work in which safety on the job is of major importance. For eight years, your company had an enviable safety record, with an accident rate far below the industry average. However, in the last two years, because the company has not upgraded the equipment used by your employees, the accident rate has soared above the industry average. Even so, the average rate for the ten years is still slightly below the industry average.

Given this, you could truthfully make the statement "Our average accident rate over the last ten years has been below the industry average." But in doing so, you would be falsely implying that your present operations are being conducted safely. You would be making an unethical statement. Were you to say "Our average accident rate over the last ten years has been *substantially* below the industry average," you would be adding the sin of exaggerating favorable data. Benjamin Franklin had it right when he said, in *Poor Richard's Almanack,* "Half the truth is often a great lie."

Don't Plagiarize

To *plagiarize* is to take the words or ideas of others and present them as your own. Much technical writing is based on research into other people's writing. It is legitimate to use other people's data and ideas, but you must give appropriate credit (see pp. 97–104). It is not legitimate to present the words and sentences of others as your own. You must quote, paraphrase, or summarize.

Seeming exceptions to this principle sometimes occur in technical writing. For example, organizations that write many proposals have large blocks of material available for use by proposal writers, such as descriptions of company facilities and equipment. Because this material, often known as "boilerplate," belongs to the organization and not the original writers, it can be used legitimately without attribution.

Construct Ethical Graphs

Like words, graphs can lie, suppress, exaggerate, and tell half-truths. The basic rule for integrity in graphs is that the physical representation of the data must accurately reflect them.[3] For example, if the number of accidents in a plant has increased and decreased only slightly over the years, the curve on the graph representing those changes should be very shallow. However, by drawing a narrow graph, a graphic artist can end up with a steep curve and thus misrepresent the changes. See Figure 7.1 for an example of an unethical bar graph.

Numbers that change in only one direction can be misrepresented by changing the physical dimensions of the graph in two directions. For example, in a bar graph, increasing the sizes of the bars both vertically and horizontally will increase the area of the bars out of proportion to the actual increases in data, thus greatly exaggerating them. Pictographs that portray physical objects, such as people and factories, often lack

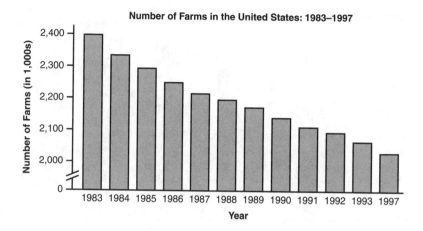

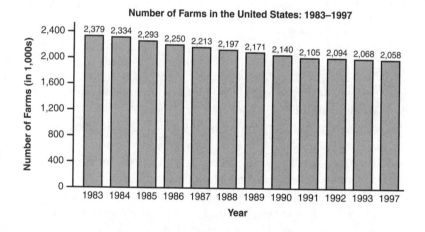

FIGURE 7.1 Vertical Misrepresentation of Data. The *top* graph greatly exaggerates the decline in family farms for the years 1983 to 1997. The *bottom* graph represents the data accurately. Also in the bottom graph, labeling each bar with the appropriate number increases the integrity of the graph.

Source: Data from U.S. Department of Commerce, *Statistical Abstract of the United States,* 118th ed. (Washington, DC: GPO, 1998) 670.

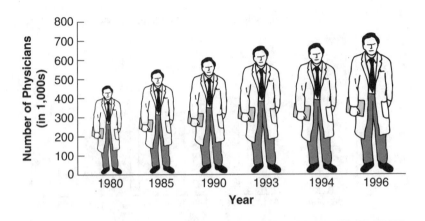

FIGURE 7.2 Inaccurate Pictograph. Because the "physician" figures in this pictograph grow in more than one dimension, they grow disproportionately to the underlying data. A well-constructed bar chart showing the same data would not be as dramatic but would represent the data accurately.

Source: Data from U.S. Department of Commerce, *Statistical Abstract of the United States,* 118th ed. (Washington, DC: GPO, 1998) 129.

integrity because they increase in two or three dimensions while the underlying numbers increase in only one (see Figure 7.2).

Because of the devaluation of the dollar caused by inflation, graphing in *current* dollars can distort the true growth in prices, wages, and such figures as the federal debt. In dealing with dollars, use *constant* dollars. In constant dollars, the value given for the dollar for a specific year is 1. All dollar values for years before and after the chosen year are then valued in proportion to the constant in a way that reflects inflation. For example, a dollar value for a year before the chosen year may have a value of 1.041, and one after may have a value of 0.984. The table in Figure 7.3 shows how this system works. The graph in Figure 7.4 demonstrates the inaccuracy of graphing in current dollars compared to graphing in constant dollars.

Inexperienced graph readers can be easily misled by unethical graphs. Experienced graph readers will spot graphs that misrepresent data and, therefore, mistrust the author of the report. You owe it to yourself and to your readers to graph ethically.

No. 771. Purchasing power of the Dollar: 1950 to 1997

[Indexes: PPI, 1982=$1.00; CPI, 1982–84=$1.00. Producer prices prior to 1961, and consumer prices prior to 1964, exclude Alaska and Hawaii. Producer prices based on finished goods index. Obtained by dividing the average price index for the 1982=100, PPI; 1982–84=100, CPI base periods (100.0) by the price index for a given period and expressing the result in dollars and cents. Annual figures are based on average monthly data]

| YEAR | ANNUAL AVERAGE AS MEASURED BY— | | YEAR | ANNUAL AVERAGE AS MEASURED BY— | | YEAR | ANNUAL AVERAGE AS MEASURED BY— | |
	Producer prices	Consumer prices		Producer prices	Consumer prices		Producer prices	Consumer prices
1950	$3.546	$4.151	1966	2.841	3.080	1982	1.000	1.035
1951	3.247	3.846	1967	2.809	2.993	1983	0.984	1.003
1952	3.268	3.765	1968	2.732	2.873	1984	0.964	0.961
1953	3.300	3.735	1969	2.632	2.726	1985	0.955	0.928
1954	3.289	3.717	1970	2.545	2.574	1986	0.969	0.913
1955	3.279	3.732	1971	2.469	2.466	1987	0.949	0.880
1956	3.195	3.678	1972	2.392	2.391	1988	0.926	0.846
1957	3.077	3.549	1973	2.193	2.251	1989	0.880	0.807
1958	3.012	3.457	1974	1.901	2.029	1990	0.839	0.766
1959	3.021	3.427	1975	1.718	1.859	1991	0.822	0.734
1960	2.994	3.373	1976	1.645	1.757	1992	0.812	0.713
1961	2.994	3.340	1977	1.546	1.649	1993	0.802	0.692
1962	2.985	3.304	1978	1.433	1.532	1994	0.797	0.675
1963	2.994	3.265	1979	1.289	1.380	1995	0.782	0.656
1964	2.985	3.220	1980	1.136	1.215	1996	0.762	0.638
1965	2.933	3.166	1981	1.041	1.098	1997	0.759	0.623

FIGURE 7.3 Purchasing Power of the Dollar: 1950–1997

Source: U.S. Department of Commerce, *Statistical Abstract of the United States,* 118th ed. (Washington, DC: GPO, 1998) Table 771.

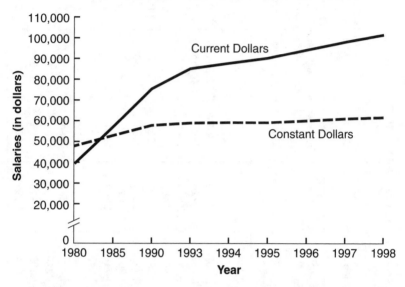

FIGURE 7.4   Comparison of Current Dollars to Constant Dollars. The curve using "Current Dollars" gives the false impression that high school superintendents have more than doubled their buying power over an 18-year period. The curve using "Constant Dollars" accurately shows that the increase was more modest than that.

Source: Data from U.S. Department of Commerce, *Statistical Abstract of the United States,* 118th ed. (Washington, DC: GPO, 1998) 176.

Don't Lie

Many of the previous principles deal with unethically shading the truth. The final principle is all encompassing: *Do not lie.* Scientists and technicians are overwhelmingly honest, but there are exceptions. A scientist has fabricated case histories to support his psychological theories. A few scientists have plagiarized the works of others. These few have been outright liars. Science and technology are built on trust. To violate that trust is to shake the very foundation on which science and technology are built.

PART TWO

The Formats of Technical Writing

8

Elements of Reports

This chapter describes every element you *might* need in a report, from the title page to the reference list. How many of these elements you actually use depends on the type of report you are writing and the needs of your audience. A large-scale company report might need every one of the elements. A short, informal, intraoffice report might need only a title page, introduction, discussion, and summary. Chapter 9, Formats of Reports, recommends the elements needed for specific kinds of reports, such as feasibility reports.

Taken together, the elements used for any particular report make up its *format*. Despite seeming arbitrary at times, formats are quite functional. For the reader, they improve accessibility, selective reading, and comprehension. For the writer, formats aid in developing a report logically. Further, the writer's knowing what each element contributes to the report makes it more likely that each element will be a useful part of the report.

Title Page

The *title page* will likely be the first thing a reader examines. It should, therefore, be useful and attractive.

To be useful, the title page should contain, at a minimum, the following information: the title of the report, the name of the author(s), the name of the person(s) for whom the report is written, and the date

Efficient, Economical Ways of Cleaning Polluted Soils and Ground Water

Prepared for
Professor James Morris
ET 232
Pollution Control Technology

By
Thelma Miller

29 February 2000

FIGURE 8.1   Basic Title Page

of the report. If those people writing and receiving the report have titles or organizational affiliations, include them, as well. Figure 8.1 shows a basic title page.

In professional situations, the title page may also include such items as contract numbers, security codes, logos, and abstracts. Generally speaking, in such situations, you will be furnished instructions or samples to work from. If in doubt, ask for help from experienced people in your organization.

The wording of the title is important. Be sure it's complete enough to make your subject clear, but do not add useless words. The title "Volcanic Gases Create Air Pollution on the Island of Hawai`i" is good because it makes clear the subject of the report and contains nothing superfluous. A title such as "Gases Create Pollution in Hawai`i" would not truly identify the subject and would almost certainly mislead the reader into thinking the subject is broader than it is. On the other hand, adding such phrases as "A Report Concerning" or "A Study of" provides no useful information.

Make your title pages attractive by keeping them uncluttered and well balanced. Don't let word-processing capabilities tempt you into using a hodgepodge of type styles and excessive ornamentation. The judicious use of some boldface type and, when appropriate, a logo will generally suffice.

Letter of Transmittal

Most technical reports go to one person or to a small group of persons. Often, a *letter of transmittal* is used to formalize the forwarding of the report. When used, the letter of transmittal gives the following basic information: a statement of transmittal, the reason for the report, and the subject and purpose of the report. If you think it's appropriate, you may also point out special features of the report (such as specially prepared charts and graphs) and acknowledge people or organizations who have been helpful in preparing it. See Figure 8.2 for an example of a typical letter of transmittal.

In some circumstances, you may point out certain implications of the report and even state your major conclusions and recommendations. How much you include in your letter of transmittal depends to some extent on whether your report includes such features as executive summaries or informative abstracts (features that will be explained

Weaver Hall
University of California
Santa Cruz, CA 95064
29 February 2000

Professor James Morris
Department of Environmental Technology
University of California
Santa Cruz, CA 95064

Dear Professor Morris:

I submit the accompanying report, "Efficient, Economical Ways of Cleaning Polluted Soils and Ground Water," in accordance with the requirements for ET 232, Pollution Control Technology.

This report describes the cleansing of polluted soils and ground water by two methods: steam injection and high-voltage electricity. In many situations, these methods are more efficient and economical than the pumping methods currently in use.

The report analyzes why corporations are not using these better techniques when they are appropriate and concludes that changes in existing state and federal environmental regulations are needed to bring about their use. Needed changes are recommended.

Sincerely,

Thelma Miller

Thelma Miller

FIGURE 8.2   Letter of Transmittal

shortly). To aid in reader accessibility and selectivity, a certain amount of redundancy is permissible and even desirable in report format, but don't overdo it.

Depending or your organization's policy, the letter of transmittal may be placed immediately before or after the title page. Alternatively, the letter of transmittal may be mailed separately as notice that the report is forthcoming.

Preface

Sometimes, reports are intended for large groups of people. For example, environmental impact statements are used to explain the environmental impacts of building large projects, such as highways. Because many people are concerned with such impacts, such reports are widely circulated. When this is the case, a *preface* is more appropriate than a letter of transmittal. A preface differs little from a letter of transmittal except in format (see Figure 8.3).

PREFACE

This report has been prepared for the California Environmental Protection Agency by the Department of Environmental Technology at the University of California at Santa Cruz. It describes the cleansing of polluted soils and ground water by two methods: steam injection and high-voltage electricity. In many situations, these methods are more efficient and cost effective than the pumping methods currently in use.

The report analyzes why California corporations are not using these better techniques when they are appropriate and concludes that changes in existing California and federal environmental regulations are needed to bring about their use. The report recommends needed changes that are in keeping with the agency's stated mission of protecting public health "in an equitable, efficient, and cost-effective manner."

FIGURE 8.3   Preface

Table of Contents

A *table of contents* (*TOC*) aids accessibility and selectivity by locating the major divisions and subdivisions within your report for readers. All division and subdivision headings in your TOC must match, word for word, the corresponding headings within the report. You may have more than three levels of headings within your report (see pp. 35–41), but generally, it's not practical for the TOC to have more than three levels. If you make your TOC overcomplicated, it will quickly become as difficult to find things in the TOC as in the report.

In constructing your TOC, use some combination of capital letters, boldface, and indentations to make the different levels of headings distinct from one another. As with the title page, however, don't be tempted

FIGURE 8.4   Table of Contents

into excessive complication by your word-processing capabilities. Figure 8.4 shows a typical TOC, suitable for a student report. You can find many other examples in the books, magazines, and journals that you read.

List of Illustrations

If you have more than three or four figures and tables in your report, you may want to include a listing of them immediately after the TOC (see Figure 8.5). If you mix tables and figures in one list, call it a *List of Illustrations*. If you have separate lists, call them *List of Tables* and *List of Figures*. You can be even more specific. For example, if you have many maps, create a *List of Maps*.

As with report titles, illustration titles should describe the illustrations adequately but not include useless language, such as "A Map Showing . . ." The reader can see it's a map. (See also Chapter 6.)

LIST OF FIGURES

		Page
2-1	Mercury Cell Replacement with Membrane Cells for Chlor-Alkali Production Facilities	2-9
2-2	Carbon Filter Bed Design	2-20
2-3	Comparison of Mercury Removal Efficiencies with Activated Carbon Injection	2-31
2-4	Equilibrium Adsorption Capacity of Elemental Mercury (Hg(O)) and Mercuric Chloride (HgCl$_2$) by a Lignite-Based Activated Carbon	2-42
4-1	Example Methodology of a Benefits Analysis	4-10
B-1	Spray Cooling System	B-12
B-2	Carbon Injection System	B-12

FIGURE 8.5   List of Figures

Source: Office of Air Quality Planning and Standards and Office of Research and Development, *An Evaluation of Mercury Control Technology and Costs,* vol. 8 of *Mercury Study Report to Congress* (Washington, DC: U.S. Environmental Protection Agency, 1997) x.

Glossary

Analyze your audience. Are you using words that are unfamiliar to your readers? If so, you will need to define those words. If you have only a few to define, you may choose to do so in the report—perhaps in the introduction or where you use the word for the first time. If you use many

---

GLOSSARY

Aquifer   An underground geologic formation, or group of formations, containing usable amounts of ground water that can supply wells and springs.

Erosion   The wearing away of soil by wind or water, intensified by land-clearing practices related to farming, residential or industrial development, road building, or logging.

Ground Water   Fresh water found underground that fills gaps between soil, sand, and gravel. It is often a major source of drinking water.

Natural Attenuation   Physical, chemical, or biological processes that act without human intervention to reduce the mass, toxicity, mobility, volume, or concentration of contaminants.

Pilot Scale   A much smaller version of the technology that would be used to treat the site.

Potentially Responsible Parties (PRPs)   The companies or individuals responsible for the cleanup of contamination at a Superfund site.

Precipitation   Removal of hazardous solids from liquid waste to permit safe disposal.

Record of Decision (ROD)   A document that announces and explains EPA's selected cleanup method(s). The ROD is based on information gathered during the remedial investigation and feasibility study and on comments received during the public comment period.

Sedimentation   Solids settled out of waste-water by gravity during treatment.

Soil Vapor   Gases that fill the spaces between soil particles.

Water Table   The level or depth of water beneath the earth's surface.

FIGURE 8.6   Glossary

Source: U.S. Environmental Protection Agency, "Superfund Fact Sheet," 1998. http://www.epa.gov/reg3hwmd/super/h&hincbu/fs0998.htm (12 January 2000).

unfamiliar words, say, as many as 10, consider using a *glossary*—that is, a list of definitions (see Figure 8.6). Glossaries typically use parallel sentence fragments as definitions, most often noun phrases. However, if the definitions are extended past the fragments, complete sentences are used. The entry for *Ground Water* in Figure 8.6 makes the concept clear. (Also see Chapter 2 for more about definitions.)

You may locate the glossary in the front of your report, probably after the TOC or the list of illustrations, or in the back as an appendix. Be sure to state in your introduction where the glossary is. Some report writers go so far as to use boldface or a symbol of some sort (such as an asterisk) to identify in the text words that are defined in the glossary.

List of Symbols

Scientific and technical writing often includes a good many symbols, most of which need definition. As with words, you can define symbols in the text of your report or in a separate list (see Figure 8.7). The *list of symbols* usually is located in the front of the report, following the list of illustrations or the glossary.

LIST OF SYMBOLS AND NOTATIONS

n	Total porosity
n_e	Effective porosity
ppm	Parts per million
TDS	Total dissolved solids
V_c	Velocity of contaminant through a control volume
V_p	Velocity of water through a control volume

FIGURE 8.7   List of Symbols and Notations

Abstracts and Summaries

The readers of technical reports are busy people. They need to have the key points of the reports they read summarized for them (see Chapters 2 and 3). *Abstracts* and *summaries* serve that purpose. Each condenses the most important facts, generalizations, conclusions, and recommendations of a report into a concise statement. Whether you call that statement an *abstract* or a *summary* depends mainly on the kind of report you are writing and where you locate the statement.

Many scientific and technical reports have a summarizing statement near the front. In that position, the statement is most often called an *abstract*. If placed at the end of the report, the statement is usually called a *summary*. Reports written specifically for executives usually contain a special kind of summary called an *executive summary*, most often placed just before the introduction. The sample report formats in Chapter 9 make clear where summaries and abstracts are placed in various kinds of reports.

Figure 8.8 is a summary found at the end of an article written for a mixed audience of generalists and specialists. It concisely restates the key facts and generalizations of the article.

Figure 8.9 is an abstract that appears before a report of scientific research. Like most abstracts, it's meant to stand alone, if need be. Therefore, it contains the key facts, generalizations, and conclusions of the report.

Figure 8.10 is an executive summary. Like many such summaries, its emphasis is on the "bottom line"—that is, the conclusions of the report.

A *descriptive abstract* is different from other abstracts and summaries. As its name implies, it describes the report. That is, rather than summarizing the report, it briefly tells what will be found in the report, thereby prompting readers to decide whether they want to read the report that follows. In a company report, the descriptive report is often placed on the title page. In a journal article, it may be placed above or below the article title, serving much like an extended title. What follows is typical:

> This article describes the usefulness of applying the principles
> of business process re-engineering to online documentation.
> Further, it presents the benefits of user-centered design, iterative
> user and task feedback, and an interdisciplinary design team.[1]

SUMMARY

Laboratory studies and field demonstrations have demonstrated the ability of steam injection to effectively recover volatile and semivoletile contaminants from the subsurface. However, in order to effectively and efficiently apply this process, it is important to characterize the site adequately to determine the horizontal and vertical distribution of the contaminant, and the preferred flow paths for the injected steam. This information is critical to the design of the steam injection and extraction system. Effective operation of the system will likely include cyclic operation of steam injection and vacuum extraction after steam breakthrough at the extraction well has occurred. Advantages of steam injection over other remediation techniques include the fact that excavation is not required, potential contaminants are not injected to the subsurface, and potentially much more rapid remediations are possible. Without a doubt, the initial capital costs for steam injection are higher than those for a system that relies on removal of soil gases without heating, such as vacuum extraction. However, the accelerated removal rates can lower the total cost of cleanup by reducing the time required for the remediation, thus reducing the overall operating costs (Udell and Stewart, 1989). In addition, the higher temperatures can increase the amount of semivolatile organics that are recovered and the removal efficiencies from clay soils by increasing the volatilization and desorption from soil surfaces. In systems where the volatilization is limited by a low volatility of the contaminant or strong adsorption onto a solid phase, the temperature of the system may actually determine the cleanup level that can be attained. There will undoubtedly be trade offs between the efficiency of the cleanup and the cost of the treatment process.

FIGURE 8.8   Summary

Source: Eva L. Davis, "Steam Injection for Soil and Aquifer Remediation," *EPA: Ground Water Issue* January 1998: 14. http://www.epa.gov/swertiol/tsp/download/steaminj (12 January 2000).

ABSTRACT

The document provides comprehensive information on the use of in situ air stripping to remediate contaminated groundwater at the U.S. Department of Energy (DOE) Savannah River site in Aiken, South Carolina. An estimated 35 million pounds of solvents were discharged from aluminum forming and metal finishing operations performed at the site between 1958 and 1985, with over 2 million pounds sent to an unlined settling basin. A pump and treat program has been ongoing since 1985 for removal of VOCs from the groundwater and a field demonstration using in situ air stripping was conducted from 1990 to 1993. The demonstration was part of a program at Savannah River to investigate the use of several technologies to enhance the pump and treat system. The in situ air stripping process increased VOC removal over conventional vacuum extraction from 109 pounds per day to 129 pounds per day. This document includes a technology description and performance report, as well as discussions of technology applicability and alternatives, cost, regulatory/policy requirements and issues, lessons learned, and references. Appendices provide more detailed information on demonstration site characteristics, technology descriptions, performance, and commercialization/intellectual property are also included.

FIGURE 8.9   Abstract

Source: "In Situ Air Stripping of Contaminated Groundwater at U.S. Department of Energy, Savannah River Site—Aiken, South Carolina," *Remediation Case Studies: Groundwater Treatment.* http://www.epa.gov/swertiol/download/remed/demorept.pdf (12 January 2000).

EXECUTIVE SUMMARY

The EPA's Robert S. Kerr Environmental Research Laboratory evaluated the following in situ technologies for remediation of dense nonaqueous phase liquids (DNAPLs) contamination occurring below the ground water table: biological, electrolytic, containment and ground modification, soil washing, air stripping, and thermal.

Remediation of DNAPLs faces challenges posed by the site stratigraphy and heterogeneity, the distribution of the contamination and the physical and chemical properties of the DNAPL. A successful technology has to be able to overcome the problems posed by the site complexity and be able to modify the properties of the DNAPL to facilitate recovery, immobilization or degradation. In addition, methodology must be adaptable to different site conditions and must be able to meet the regulatory goals.

Thermally based technologies are regarded as among the most promising, with steam enhanced extraction (SEE) as probably the most promising candidate. The next group of promising technologies are the soil washing technologies because they can manipulate chemical equilibria and reduce capillary forces. A blend of alkalis, cosolvents and surfactants is probably the best combination for a soil washing application, each important for its own reasons. Alkalis can saponify certain DNAPLs and affect wetability and sorption; cosolvents provide viscous stability and enhance solubility and mass transfer between the aqueous phase and the DNAPL; surfactants have the largest impacts on solubility and interfacial tension reduction. Water flooding is best applied in highly contaminated areas as a precursor to these methods.

The thermal and soil washing technologies are considered as best suited for areas that are highly contaminated with DNAPLs. However, these techniques by themselves still may not be able to achieve the currently mandated regulated cleanup standards. Thus, consideration should be given to using these technologies in combination with the technologies suitable for long-term plume management. The bioremediation techniques and permeable treatment walls hold the best promise.

FIGURE 8.10 Executive Summary

Source: Adapted from William H. Engelmann, "DNAPL Technologies Evaluated," *Ground Water Currents* April 1995: 1. http://www.epa.gov/swertio1/products/newsltrs/gwc/gwcdnapl.htm (15 January 2000).

Introduction

Before reading what follows, read the *introduction* in Figure 8.11. Have it in mind as you read this section.

An introduction *must do* these two things:

- Announce the subject of the report.
- Announce the purpose of the report.

An introduction *may do* any of these four things:

- Catch the reader's interest in the article or report.
- Define terms and concepts.
- Provide theoretical and historical background.
- Forecast the content and organization of the report.

How many of the optional things your introduction does depends on your audience and plan for your report or article. For a general, nontechnical audience, you would likely begin with something to catch the reader's interest. If your report or article uses words and concepts that the audience will need defined and explained to understand your subject matter, you may choose to provide the definitions and explanations in the introduction. However, you may also choose to provide

---

INTRODUCTION

This document contains detailed information on how steam injection can be used to recover organic contaminants from the subsurface, the contaminant and subsurface conditions for which the process may be appropriate, and general design and equipment considerations. In addition, laboratory and field-scale experiments are described, and available treatment cost information is provided. This document is not meant to provide detailed information that would allow the design of a steam injection remediation project, but rather to provide design considerations to familiarize remediation workers with what is involved in the process.

FIGURE 8.11   Introduction to Journal Article

Source: Adapted from Eva L. Davis, "Steam Injection for Soil and Aquifer Remediation," *EPA: Ground Water Issue* January 1998: 1. http://www.epa.gov/swertiol/tsp/download/steaminj (12 January 2000).

them elsewhere in the article, perhaps where you use each word or concept. The same holds true for providing needed theoretical and historical background.

If your report is complex, you would be wise to forecast its content and organization. For a short, uncomplicated report or article, you could probably forego this step, but it would always be appropriate to include it.

No matter what else you *may* do in your introduction, you *must* always announce your subject and purpose. In other words, tell your readers what you are talking about and why.

Introductions to articles aimed at general audiences tend to emphasize interest catching and to be more informal than introductions aimed at specialized audiences. In these general-audience introductions, the subject and purpose will be announced but perhaps somewhat indirectly. Figure 8.12 illustrates such an introduction. It asks questions that

---

INTRODUCTION

Why is there still water that's too dirty for swimming, fishing, or drinking? Why are native species of plants and animals disappearing from many rivers, lakes, and coastal waters?

The United States has made tremendous advances in the past 25 years to clean up the aquatic environment by controlling pollution from industries and sewage treatment plants. Unfortunately, we did not do enough to control pollution from diffuse, or nonpoint, sources. Today, nonpoint source (NPS) pollution remains the Nation's largest source of water quality problems. It's the main reason that approximately 40 percent of our surveyed rivers, lakes, and estuaries are not clean enough to meet basic uses such as fishing or swimming.

NPS pollution occurs when rainfall, snowmelt, or irrigation runs over land or through the ground, picks up pollutants, and deposits them into rivers, lakes, and coastal waters or introduces them into ground water. Imagine the path taken by a drop of rain from the time it hits the ground to when it reaches a river, ground water, or the ocean. Any pollutant it picks up on its journey can become part of the NPS problem. NPS pollution also includes adverse changes to the vegetation, shape, and flow of streams and other aquatic systems.

FIGURE 8.12   Introduction for a General Audience

Source: Nonpoint Source Pollution: The Nation's Largest Water Quality Problem. http://www.epa.gov/qwow/nps/facts/point1.htm (12 January 2000).

remind the reader that serious environmental problems still exist. Some inference is required of the reader, but it's clear that the subject will be a kind of pollution known rather awkwardly as *nonpoint source pollution*, and the purpose will be to describe where such pollution occurs and how it affects the environment.

Creating interest-catching introductions like the one in Figure 8.12 is appropriate for a general audience; just don't get too breathless about it.

Discussion

The *discussion*, where you fulfill your subject and purpose, will be the longest part of your article or report. How you organize and write it will depend on your purpose and audience. For direction, see Chapters 1 through 7 and remember the seven principles of technical writing:

1. Know your purpose.
2. Know your audience.
3. Choose and organize your content around your purpose and audience.
4. Write clearly and precisely.
5. Use good page design.
6. Think visually.
7. Write ethically.

Conclusions and Recommendations

Analytical reports require *conclusions*. Recommendation reports require *conclusions* and *recommendations*. *Conclusions* are opinions based on the data in reports. For example, a recent journal article analyzed data that indicate that ulcers are caused by bacteria—not stress, as previously thought. The last paragraph of the article expressed a conclusion based on the data:

Meanwhile, the future of current ulcer sufferers looks brighter than ever. Says consensus team member Ann L. B. Williams, M.D., of George Washington University Medical College, "We now have an opportunity to cure a disease that previously we had only been able to suppress or control."[2]

Whereas *conclusions* are opinions based on the data presented, *recommendations* are the actions recommended (or recommended against) based on the conclusions. Recommendation reports, often called *feasibility reports,* are common in business and government organizations. The studies that lead to such reports examine problems. For example, researchers working for a state prison system may be asked to look for ways to reduce the increasing pressure on prison facilities caused by growing prison populations. After due study, the researchers may reach a conclusion such as this one:

A major conclusion, based on our data, is that society and nonviolent offenders might be better served by having such offenders perform community service over several years rather than serve prison terms. Removing nonviolent offenders from the prison population would help reduce the overcrowding that exists.

Based on such a conclusion, the researchers then make a recommendation, such as this:

We recommend legislation allowing and encouraging judges to sentence nonviolent offenders to long-term community service, rather than prison. The legislation should authorize follow-up research to analyze the value of the community service and its effect on the recidivism rate of those sentenced to such service.

Because conclusions are opinions and because recommendations are based on conclusions, be sure the conclusions you reach are well grounded on reliable data.

If you have more than a few conclusions, you might help your reader by listing and even rating them, as is done in Figure 8.13.

CONCLUSIONS

The following conclusions are presented in approximate order of degree of certainty in the conclusion, based on the quality of the underlying database. The conclusions progress from those with greater certainty to those with lesser certainty.

- Conversion of mercury cell chlor-alkali plants to a mercury-free process is technically feasible and has been previously demonstrated.

- Energy conservation and switching to low-mercury fuels would reduce the amount of mercury being emitted by utility boilers.

- Injection of activated carbon into the flue gas of MWC's and MWI's can achieve mercury reductions of at least 85 percent. The addition of activated carbon to the flue gas of these source types would not have a significant impact on the amount of particulate matter requiring disposal.

- Numerous opportunities exist for replacing mercury in various products with other materials, such as solid state electronics for mercury switches, digital thermometers for mercury thermometers and zinc air batteries for mercury batteries.

- Removing mercury-containing products such as batteries, fluorescent lights and thermostats from the waste stream can reduce the mercury input to waste combustors without lowering the energy content of the waste stream. The mercury removal efficiency would vary, however, depending on the extent of the separation.

- Selenium filters are a demonstrated technology in Sweden for control of mercury emissions from lead smelters. Carbon filter beds have been used successfully in Germany for mercury control on utility boilers and MWC's. These technologies have not been demonstrated in the U.S.

- Control technologies designed for control of pollutants other than mercury (e.g., acid gases and particulate matter) vary in their mercury-removal capability, but in general achieve reductions no greater than 50 percent

- The available data on coal cleaning indicate that mercury reductions ranged from zero to 64 percent. The average reduction was 21 percent. This variation may be due to several factors including different cleaning methods, different mercury concentrations in the raw coal and different mercury analytical techniques. There are no data available to assess the potential for mercury emissions from coal-cleaning slurries.

FIGURE 8.13   Conclusions Stated in List

Source: Office of Air Quality Planning and Standards and Office of Research and Development, *An Evaluation of Mercury Control Technology and Costs,* vol. 8 of *Mercury Study Report to Congress* (Washington, DC: U.S. Environmental Protection Agency, 1997) 6-1.

Appendixes

As their name indicates, *appendixes* are items appended to the main body of a report. They are excellent devices to help satisfy the needs of a dual audience for a report. For example, suppose the prison feasibility study described in the preceding section has two audiences: legislators and legislative aides. The legislators will want to know the salient facts and the conclusions and recommendations reached. They will not want to be buried under accounts of research methods and the like. However, the legislative aides may need such information to evaluate the study. Putting the detailed information in an appendix makes it available for the aides but out the way of the legislators.

You can make two mistakes in selecting material for an appendix. You may segregate material in the appendix that everyone in your audience needs and wants and, therefore, run the risk of it being overlooked. Conversely, you may load your appendix with material that nobody needs or wants, increasing the bulk of your report but not its value. As always, let your audience and purpose guide you in reaching such decisions.

Documentation

Most technical reports require *documentation:* the use of references to identify material you relied on in preparing the report. References credit your sources and allow your readers to find them, if they wish. Many documentation systems exist. If you are preparing an article for a journal, you need to obtain the style book used by that journal as a guide to its documentation system. Likewise, companies, government agencies, university departments, and so forth may all require some special systems of documentation.

It all seems a bit bewildering, but most documentation systems require the same information: author's name, editor's name (if any), title of book or article, and publication data. Publication data in the case of a book include the publisher's name, city of publication, and date of publication. When necessary, publication data may also include such information as edition numbers, volume numbers, and series numbers. Publication data for an article would include the page numbers of the article and the name, volume, number, and date of the periodical.

The differences in documentation systems involve mainly differences in punctuation, capitalization, and the order in which information is presented. The best way to learn a system is to obtain the style book involved and, when you are documenting your report, imitate the appropriate formats down to the last period. Meanwhile, pay attention to what you are seeing and doing, particularly to punctuation, capitalization, and order.

Provided here are samples based on *The Chicago Manual of Style's* author-date system. It is used in many of the natural and physical sciences and in some of the social sciences. It is, therefore, a common system. It is also, as documentation systems go, a fairly simple one.[3] You will find here enough samples to see you through a typical report. If you need more than is provided, see *The Manual* itself, readily available in most libraries.

Documentation using the author-date system requires adding author-date references in the text that refer the reader to an alphabetized list called by such titles as *References* or *Works Cited.* Place each author-date reference within parentheses in the text, as illustrated in Figure 8.14. The actual format depends on the information you have to provide, as illustrated here. As you use these samples, carefully note punctuation, capitalization, and order:

Photoperiod regulation may also have other notable consequences. In several conifers, early flushing after short-day (SD) treatment has been reported (for example, Bigras and D'Aoust 1993; Dormling 1968.) According to Grossnickle (1991), SD treatment also increased the root growth capacity of western hemlock seedlings at low root temperature.

FIGURE 8.14   Author-Date References within Text

Source: Adapted from Jaana Luoranen and Risto Rikala, "Growth Regulation and Cold Hardening of Silver Birch Seedlings with Short-Day Treatment," *Tree Planters' Notes* 48 (1997): 65.

Basic Format

(Baker 1998)

Reference to Specific Page or Division

(Baker 1998, 74)
(Baker 1998, Ch. 9)

Reference to Volume

(Cornwall 1999, vol. 2)

Reference to Volume and Page

(Cornwall 1999, 2:67)

Two or Three Authors

(Fielding and Meaders 1996)
(Manchester, Kehoe, and Holl 1998)

More Than Three Authors

(Osborn and others 1993)

Author with Two or More Works of Same Date Cited

(Larsen, *Generic drugs,* 1998)
(Larsen, *Generic painkillers,* 1998)

Organization as Author

(Landings Corporation 1996)

Multiple References in Same Parentheses

(Baker 1998; Lewis 1993; Noelani 1995)

Author's Name Used in Text

(2000)
(2000, 74)

Note: When you cite authors directly in text, do not repeat their names in parenthetical references (see Figure 8.14).

REFERENCES

Baskin, H. 1999. Telephone conversation with author, 18 August.

Boberg, T. C. 1988. *Thermal methods of oil recovery.* New York: Wiley.

Davis, E. L. Steam injection for soil and aquifer remediation. *EPA: Ground Water Issue* January 1998: 1. http://www.epa.gov/swertiol/tsp/download/steaminj (12 January 2000).

Itamura, M. T., and K. S. Udell. 1995. An analysis of optimal cycling time and ultimate chlorinated hydrocarbon removal from heterogeneous media using cyclic steam injection. *Proceedings of the ASME Heat Transfer and Fluids Engineering Divisions* HTD-321: 57–62.

Keyes, B. R., and G. D. Silcox. 1994. Fundamental study of the thermal desorption of toulene from montmorillonite clay particles. *Environmental Science Technology* 28: 840–49.

FIGURE 8.15   **Reference List**

Figure 8.15 illustrates how to construct an alphabetized reference list. Here are examples of typical entries for such a list:

Basic Book

Winchester, S. 1999. *The professor and the madman.* New York: HarperCollins.

Note: This entry lists, in order, the author, date, title, city of publication, and publisher. You may use initials or full names of authors, but be consistent throughout the reference list. The names of publishing companies are usually given in short forms. For example, *HarperCollins Publishers, Inc.* is listed as *HarperCollins*.

Book with Two or More Authors

> Spoehr, K. T., and S. W. Lehmkuble. 1982. *Visual information processing.* San Francisco: W. H. Freeman.

Note: Do not use "and others" in a reference list. List all the authors—last name first for the first author, and normal order for the rest.

Book with Editor

> Frank, F. W., and P. A. Treichler, eds. 1989. *Language, gender, and professional writing.* New York: MLA.

Note: Use *ed.* for *editor, eds.* for two or more *editors,* and *trans.* for singular or plural *translators.* Names of organizations likely to be known to readers are often abbreviated—in this case, *MLA* for the *Modern Language Association.*

Organization as Author

> Department of Agriculture (DOA). 1999. *National forestry manual.* Washington, DC: GPO.

Note: *GPO* is a widely used abbreviation for the *Government Printing Office,* which prints most books published by the federal government.

Later Edition

> Fuller, Jane. 1999. *The history of Skidaway Island.* 2d ed. Savannah, GA: Pilgrim Press.

Note: When the city of publication is not well known, use additional identification, such as the state abbreviation.

Essay in an Edited Collection

> Cooper, M. 1989. The ecology of writing. In *Writing as social action,* ed. M. M. Cooper and M. Holzman. 1–13. Portsmouth, NH: Boynton/Cook Heinemann.

Basic Journal Entry

> Cushman, J. 1999. Critical literacy and institutional language. *Research in the Teaching of English* 33: 245–74.

Note: This entry lists, in order, the author, date, article, journal, volume, and inclusive pages for the article. Use this form for journals that are paginated by volume, rather than issue. Treat the names of multiple authors for articles as you do multiple authors for books. Cite page numbers as in these examples:

1–13; 16–28; 200–206; 201–8; 224–29; 1156–68.

Entry for Journals Paginated by Issue

Hall, L. 1999. Taking charge of menopause. *FDA Consumer,* 33, no. 6. (November–December): 17–21.

Note: Use the issue number and the date in the journal masthead—for example, *December, Fall, 18 June,* and so forth. Put *no.* (for *number*) to distinguish the issue number from the volume number.

Entry for Popular Magazine

Boyer, Peter J. 2000. DNA on trial. *The New Yorker,* 17 January, 42–53.

Paper Read at a Meeting

Colomb, G. G., and J. Simutis. 1992. Written conversation and the transition to college. Paper presented at the Computers and Writing Conference, May, Ann Arbor, MI.

Personal Communication

Cunningham, D. 1999. E-mail to author, 28 October.

Note: Identify the nature of the communication: letter, telephone call, e-mail, interview, and so forth.

Two Entries for an Author

Eisner, E. W. 1985. *The educational imagination.* 2d ed. New York: Macmillan.

———. 1991. *The enlightened eye.* New York: Macmillan.

Note: Use three long dashes (or six hyphens) for another entry by the same author.

Internet Documentation

Given the vast and ever-changing nature of the Internet, citing sources found online can be a challenge. Authors' names may be lacking or abbreviated. Articles may not be named. Because of revisions, dates of publication may change frequently or be missing altogether. Many Internet sources are not paginated.

Therefore, when you compile Internet citations in your list of references, you will need to use different forms than you use for books and articles. Despite the differences in form, however, the purposes are the same: to give credit to the original source and to enable the reader to locate the source.

The system shown here is based on the *Columbia Guide to Online Style*[4]—a source endorsed by the Alliance for Computers and Writing—and *The Chicago Manual*'s citation style. The basic parts of the citations used in this system are as follow but always subject to availability and applicability:

- Author's name, last name first (If there is more than one author, put the names of subsequent authors in normal order.) If only the author's alias or log-in name is available, use that. If no identifier is available for the author, use the best information you have, such as the name of the document or site.
- Title of document and title of complete work
- Volume, version, or file number
- Last date of document
- Access information
- Date accessed

The following examples illustrate the use of this system for several different kinds of sources (see also Figure 8.15):

World Wide Web (WWW) Site

Thomas Crapper: Myth & reality. 1993. *Plumbing and Mechanical Magazine*. http://www.theplumber.com/ crapper.html (10 November 1999).

File Transfer Protocol (FTP)

Irons, Mary, and Geoffrey Manchester. 10 August 1999. The vault of the Sidney Opera House. ftp://ftp.cchs.su.edu.au/ (5 January 2000).

Listserv

AliceB. 12 December 1999. Re: trigeminal neuralgia. TN-L Trigemnal & Facial Neuralgia. tnl@listserv.uark.edu (6 February 2000).

E-mail

Cunningham, D. 1999. E-mail to author, 28 October.

Construct parenthetical author-date references in your text for Internet citations just as you do for other forms of publication (see pp. 98–99). As with books and articles, the actual format of the parenthetical Internet reference depends on the information you have. For example, the reference in your text for the listserv citation above would be as follows:

(AliceB 1999)

Copyright

Copyright laws protect most published work. Exceptions are most materials published by the United States government and state and local governments. Such work is normally not copyrighted.

If your work will be unpublished—for example, a student report— you must identify your sources, but you do not need permission to use copyrighted material. In general, if you plan to publish your work, you must get permission from the copyright holders (usually, the publishers) to use figures and extended quotations from copyrighted works. See *The Chicago Manual of Style* concerning copyright law.

9

Formats of Reports

Business and professional people write an assortment of reports. In these reports, they instruct, analyze information, propose work to be done, report progress on work, and report and interpret the results of research. This chapter describes how to format this variety of reports.

Instructions

Most instructions have a basic three-part format: an introduction, a list of equipment and materials needed, and how-to instructions. If you have ever followed a recipe in cooking or built a model airplane, the format will be immediately familiar to you. Many instructions also include warnings, theory, and a glossary.

Introduction

An introduction to instructions must announce the subject and purpose of the instructions, something like this:

> Leaking faucets waste water, stain the sink, and create annoying dripping sounds. With the right equipment, stopping the leak is a simple process.

This simple introduction makes clear that the subject is *stopping a faucet leak* and the purpose is to show you how to do it. In addition, this introduction provides motivation for doing the task—stop waste, staining, and annoying sounds.

If the process you are going to describe is complex, you might also preview it:

> The process involves turning off the water to the faucet, disassembling the faucet, replacing the faucet washer, reassembling the faucet, and turning the water on again.

You may also include such things as warnings, references to a glossary, and definitions, but in general, keep introductions uncomplicated.

List of Equipment and Materials

People about to do a task need to know what they must have to complete the task. A list detailing the needed equipment and materials provides the necessary information:

- A box of washers of assorted sizes
- A screwdriver
- An adjustable wrench

How much information you provide in your list depends on your audience analysis. If your analysis tells you that your readers are experienced tool users, the simple list above should be sufficient. If you have inexperienced tool users, you may have to expand the list:

- A screwdriver of the appropriate type and size. Screws have either straight-blade slots or phillips slots (see Figure 1). The screwdriver must match the slot. In either case, the screwdriver blade must fit securely into the slot of the screw without slippage (see Figure 2).

As this expanded list indicates, figures (not shown here) make clear the distinction between a straight-blade slot and a phillips slot and how the screwdriver blade should fit the slot. As Chapter 6, Think Visually, emphasizes, when pictures are clearer than words, use pictures.

Sometimes, you may find that your readers need a rather complete description of a tool or mechanism involved in a process. In describing mechanisms or tools, you can include information on their purpose and function, parts and subparts, purpose and function of the parts and subparts, construction, materials, appearance, size, color, and so forth. You can also describe how to use the mechanism safely. How much of this sort of information you include depends, as always, on what your readers actually need. Figure 9.1 provides a good example of such a description. Again, notice the use of illustrations in the description.

If you think it's necessary, you can also include information about where materials and equipment can be obtained, what they cost, and so forth. Tell your readers what they need to know to do the job properly.

How-To Instructions

Figure 9.2 illustrates a partial list of how-to instructions. Look at it now, before you continue with the text. As Figure 9.2 demonstrates, how-to instructions follow these principles:

- Each instruction of process presented separately and in chronological order
- Use of simple language, active voice, and imperative mood: "Loosen packing nut with wrench"
- Use of clarifying illustrations
- Inclusion of helpful advice: "Most nuts loosen by turning counter-clockwise"

Although how-to instructions are not always numbered (as in Figure 9.2), they frequently are.

It's critically important in writing how-to instructions to break the process down into manageable instructions. An instruction may include only one step (as in instruction 3 in Figure 9.2) or several (as in instructions 1 and 2). When you include more than one step in an instruction, be sure they are all closely related.

If you are experienced in the process being described, you may unintentionally leave out steps that you have come to do almost automatically, without thinking about them. Be sure to think through the entire process, step by step; leave out nothing that your audience analysis tells

Portable Power Circular Saws

The portable power circular saw can save you "muscle power" and time (fig. 12). You can rent or buy one. It may be used as a crosscut saw or a ripsaw—depending upon the type of blade used.

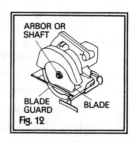

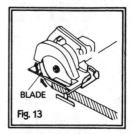

Fig. 12

The *saw blade* should be adjusted so that the amount of blade that extends below the "shoe" is slightly greater (1/16 to 1/8 inch) than the thickness of material to be cut. As you guide the saw forward, the blade is exposed for cutting (fig. 13).

For ripping work, circular saws come with a "ripping guide." After adjusting the blade, set the ripping guide the same distance from the saw as the width of the material to be cut off.

Fig. 13

Then place the guide against the edge of the piece as you cut (fig. 14).

For crosscutting, or cutting off material, turn the ripping guide upside down, so that it will be out of the way. Using a framing square and pencil, draw a line to mark where to cut. Then guide the saw blade carefully along the line.

Fig. 14

Using a portable power saw can save much time and effort. For safety and the proper use of the saw, follow these steps:

1. Make sure that the saw you use is equipped with a guard that will automatically adjust in use so that none of the teeth are exposed above the work.

2. Make sure the saw is equipped with an automatic power cutoff button.

3. Always wear goggles or face mask when using a power saw.

4. Carefully examine the material and make certain that it is free of nails or other metal before you start cutting.

5. Grasp the saw with both hands and hold it firmly against the work.

6. Never overload the saw motor by pushing too hard or cutting material that is too thick for this small saw.

7. Always try to make a straight cut to keep from binding the saw blade. If it does bind, back the saw out slowly and firmly in a straight line. As you continue with the cutting, adjust the direction of the cut so that you are cutting in a straight line.

8. Always pull the electric plug before you make any adjustments to the saw or inspect the blade.

FIGURE 9.1   Mechanism Description

Source: U.S. Department of Agriculture, *Simple Home Repairs: Outside* (Washington, DC: GPO, 1986) 6.

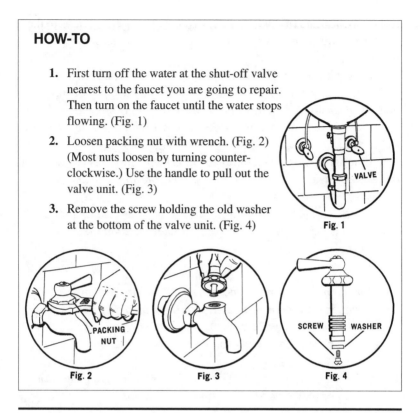

HOW-TO

1. First turn off the water at the shut-off valve nearest to the faucet you are going to repair. Then turn on the faucet until the water stops flowing. (Fig. 1)

2. Loosen packing nut with wrench. (Fig. 2) (Most nuts loosen by turning counter-clockwise.) Use the handle to pull out the valve unit. (Fig. 3)

3. Remove the screw holding the old washer at the bottom of the valve unit. (Fig. 4)

Fig. 1

Fig. 2   **Fig. 3**   **Fig. 4**

FIGURE 9.2   How-To Instructions

Source: U.S. Department of Agriculture, *Simple Home Repairs: Inside* (Washington, DC: GPO, 1986) 1.

you your reader needs. A good check is to have someone of the skill level you expect in your audience perform the process following your in-structions. Gaps in your instructions will show up quickly when you do.

Warnings

To protect consumers from injury and to protect companies from expen-sive lawsuits, warnings are given extensively in instructions. They may stand out in a separate section of their own or be part of the introduc-tion, list of equipment and materials, or how-to instructions. Manufacturers have learned (to their sorrow) that risks that seem obvious to them are not obvious to everyone. Err on the side of too many warnings, not on too few.

Make your warnings stand out so that no one will miss them. Box them; use a larger, distinctive, or different-colored typeface; use symbols, such as an exclamation point or a skull and crossbones. When the risk involved might lead to death or serious injury, use all three techniques.

Although there is not complete agreement on levels of warnings, three levels have become common: *Caution, Warning,* and *Danger:*

- Use *Caution* to warn against actions that may lead to undesirable results but that are not likely to damage equipment or injure people:

Caution

If you have external devices, such as an external hard drive, connected to your computer, turn them on before you turn on your computer. Failure to do so may keep your computer from recognizing them when you do turn them on.

- Use *Warning* to warn against actions that may damage equipment or materials or cause mild injury to users:

WARNING
This process will erase all information on this disk.

- Use *Danger* to warn against actions that may result in serious injury or death:

DANGER!
Do not stand on the top two steps or the top of this
stepladder. Doing so may result in a fall that
could cause serious injury or death.

Theory

Sometimes, users of instructions may benefit from knowing the theory that underlies the instructions. Knowing the theory may clarify the procedures described or motivate users to follow the instructions. In the following example, the author of instructions meant for managers of seedling nurseries explains the theory underlying the instructions:

> Managers of container seedling nurseries sow multiple seeds per cell to increase the probability of having at least one germinant per cell. This ensures that their greenhouses are fully stocked so that seedling contracts may be filled. However, this practice wastes valuable seed and necessitates thinning extra germinants at an additional cost. Multiple sowing, therefore, should be minimized.
>
> Many factors influence how many seeds per cell to sow, including species, seed size, seed availability and cost, type and accuracy of sowing equipment, sowing and thinning labor costs, and germination data reliability. The primary factor, however, is greenhouse germination percentage. When germination percentage is known or assumed, nursery managers use various rules of thumb or rely on the probability tables found in Tinus and McDonald (1979) to determine the number of expected empty cells. These tables are complete but sometimes cumbersome and currently unavailable to new managers.
>
> Fortunately, the percentage of empty cells can be obtained using a hand-held calculator (Schwartz 1993). Taking this procedure one step farther, the probability tables of Tinus and McDonald (1979), showing both filled and empty cells, can be recreated on a personal computer.[1]

If the theory you present is lengthy, you may want to put it in a section by itself. Most of the time, however, you will present theory as part of your introduction, as was the case in the previous example. Include theory in instructions only if you are reasonably sure your readers will benefit from it.

Glossary

Occasionally, you will use enough words unfamiliar to your readers to justify including a glossary with your instructions. When such is the case, construct your glossary following the instructions on pages 86–87. You may place your glossary at the beginning or the end of your instructions. In either case, refer the reader to it in your introduction.

Analytical Reports

Analytical reports analyze data to arrive at conclusions. Some reports go one step further and recommend that actions be taken or not taken, based on the conclusions reached. If the person making the report has the authority to do so, the report might state a decision. Therefore, analytical reports may also be known as *recommendation reports* or *decision reports*. When the purpose of the report is to examine the feasibility of some plan of action, it may also be called a *feasibility report*.

The executives of organizations are constantly making decisions based on answers to questions such as these:

What can be done about the high absentee rate in our Charleston plant?

What is the sales potential of our new VCR?

Which health plan should we choose for our company?

The answers to such questions are most often given in analytical reports. When the report is simple and short, it is usually presented in a memorandum or letter. (These types of reports are discussed in Chapter 10, Formats of Correspondence.) When the report is complex and long, it needs more structure, such as a title page, table of contents, and summary. These additional elements are not added to increase the weight and formality of the report; rather, they are added to help readers find their way through the report. (Chapter 8, Elements of Reports, provides the information you need to construct the elements of long reports. Here, the discussion is about how to put the elements into an appropriate format.)

Format

Depending on your purpose, the needs of your readers, and the content itself, analytical reports will use formats such as the following:

Format I	**Format II**
Title page	Title page
Table of contents	Table of contents
Executive summary	Introduction
Introduction	Summary
Discussion	Conclusions
Conclusions	Recommendations
Recommendations	Discussion

In Format I, although the executive summary highlights major conclusions and recommendations, the emphasis falls on the discussion. In Format II, the discussion is deemphasized and the summary, conclusions and recommendations are brought to the forefront.

Both are good formats. The one you would choose would depend on your needs and those of your readers. For example, you might know that your readers will be skeptical of your conclusions, and, therefore, wish to emphasize your discussion by choosing Format I. Or you might know that your readers will prefer seeing the big picture first, and, therefore, choose Format II. To formats like I and II, you can add, as needed, such elements as lists of illustrations, glossaries, documentation, and appendixes (all explained in Chapter 8, Elements of Reports).

Discussion sections of analytical reports can be rather specialized, depending on the questions being examined. The following should help you sort things out.

Discussion Sections

Discussion sections in analytical reports tend to use one of the following organizations: *classical argument, pro and con, choice of alternatives,* or *problem/solution.* No matter which organization you choose, your discussion has to build a firm base for the conclusions, recommendations, and decisions that follow from it.

In a *classical argument* format, you would support a large opinion by a series of smaller opinions, which are in turn supported by facts. In argument, the large opinion is called the *major premise;* the smaller opinions are called *minor premises.* Your discussion format might look like this:

Major premise

Minor premise A

Factual support

Minor premise B

Factual support

Minor premise C

Factual support

In an actual argument, your format might look like this:

Fusion energy has the potential to be a major source of energy in the twenty-first century.

- Fuel for fusion energy is easily available and virtually inexhaustible.

  Factual support

- Fusion energy does not produce the pollutants that lead to global warming.

  Factual support

- Fusion energy is a safer source of power than present-day nuclear power plants.

  Factual support[2]

Other forms of argument are all variations of the classical argument format.

If existing opinions and facts weigh against the major premise, it's both ethical and convincing to use a *pro and con* argument. (*Ethical* because you are not hiding anything. *Convincing* because you're perceived not to be hiding anything.) A pro and con argument weighs the points in favor of something (*pros*) against the points opposed (*cons*), resulting in this format:

A statement or a question
  Pro: Opinions and facts supporting the affirmative
  Con: Opinions and facts supporting the negative

An actual pro and con argument might break out like this:

Fusion energy has the potential to be a major source of energy in the twenty-first century.

Pros

- Fuel for fusion energy is easily available and virtually inexhaustible.

  Factual support

- Fusion energy does not produce the pollutants that lead to global warming.

  Factual support

- Fusion energy is a safer source of power than present-day nuclear power plants.

  Factual support

Cons

- Although fusion energy is safer than fission energy, it does produce high-energy neutrons that induce radioactivity, leaving problems of radioactive waste.

  Factual support

- The cost of fusion energy is too high for it to be a practical source of power.

  Factual support

Even if you think the *pro* side of the argument is the right side, to present an ethical argument, you should still include the *cons*. However, it is perfectly ethical to point out ways in which mitigating facts or circumstances weaken the *con* side. For example, evidence suggests that, with the right technology, the cost of fusion energy could be comparable to that of fossil fuels.

After weighing the pros and cons for your readers, you will be expected, of course, to arrive at a conclusion: Yes or no? Fusion energy has the potential to be a major source of energy in the twenty-first century.

Frequently, an analytical discussion calls for a *choice of alternatives*. You might be called on to make a recommendation concerning some major company purchase—for example, vans to make company deliveries. In a choice-of-alternatives plan, you have to deal with the alternatives available and the criteria by which you judge the alternatives. *Criteria* are the standards you use to judge something. In the case of vans, you might have as alternatives all the vans made by major truck manufacturers. The criteria might concern initial cost, operating cost, carrying capacity, and maintenance record. You can organize your discussion by either alternatives or criteria:

By Alternatives	*By Criteria*
Van A	Initial cost
Initial cost	Van A
Operating cost	Van B
Carrying capacity	Operating cost
Maintenance record	Van A
Van B	Van B
Initial cost	Carrying capacity
Operating cost	Van A
Carrying capacity	Van B
Maintenance record	Maintenance record
	Van A
	Van B

Organizing by alternatives has the advantage of offering a complete discussion of each van in one section. Organizing by criteria has the advantage of allowing for selective reading; that is, some readers may be more interested in cost than carrying capacity. Organizing by criteria allows them to find and read the section they are most concerned with. Both plans are good. As usual, your purpose and audience will help you choose the one suited to your situation.

In the first part of a *problem/solution* discussion, define the problem. Use the available data to demonstrate that a problem really exists. For example, suppose you are an executive with a computer company that has a problem with its technical help line. Customers who call it get repeated busy signals. And after connecting to the help line, they may have waits up to an hour. To define the problem, you answer questions like these:

Typically, how many times does a buyer of one of your computers call in seeking help?

How many calls a day does your help line receive?

How many technical support consultants does the company have?

What is the cost to your company of running the help line?

Can the company afford to increase the service to an acceptable level and keep its profit margin high enough to stay in business?

How is the problem damaging customer relations?

and so forth

After you define the problem, offer your solution. If there are criteria you must apply to any solution, clearly state them. For example, in the technical help line problem, a criterion might be that the solution must be affordable to the company. A solution that cut too heavily into company profit margins—such as hiring large numbers of consultants—would not be acceptable. Perhaps in this case, your solution might be to allow calls only to customers who buy service policies with their computers. The money from the service policies would pay for an expanded and acceptable technical help line.

After stating your solution, you would need to demonstrate its likely effectiveness. Again, you would be using your data to answer questions:

Have other companies tried this approach?

How successful have they been?

How much money is needed to expand the help line to an acceptable level of service?

How much would a service policy have to cost?

How would consumers react to buying such a policy?

and so forth

Your discussion has to show the strong likelihood of your solution being successful.

If you offer more than one solution, the solution portion of the report might use a choice-of-alternatives plan. In this case, you might offer two alternatives: a service policy and pay-as-you-go. In the pay-as-you-go plan, the customer would pay for each help call made. You might then compare the alternatives using criteria such as customer acceptance, ease of administration, and effect on profit margin. At the end of your discussion, you could weigh the evidence in a series of conclusions and recommend which solution the company should choose.

Using the various forms of argument to analyze a set of facts, you can carefully build a powerful case for your position. But remember that, ultimately, your analysis can be no better than your facts. Also remember that, even though you may be trying to convince your readers to accept your point of view, it is your responsibility to argue ethically. Do not, for example, slant your facts one way or the other.

(See Appendix A for a sample analytical report.)

Proposals

In a proposal, one organization (or sometimes an individual) offers, for a price, its services to another organization. For example, Organization X, a research organization, may offer to research and offer a solution to a problem that Organization Y has. Or Company A, a computer software manufacturer, may offer to research the software needs of Company B and offer to install the software needed to satisfy those needs. A *proposal* is essentially a specialized form of argument and uses many of the techniques discussed in the previous section.

Proposals are either *solicited* or *unsolicited*. In a solicited proposal, an organization in need of services advertises its needs in a document called a *request for proposal* (*RFP*). The RFP will state the needs and request that organizations that can satisfy those needs submit proposals. The RFP will usually state quite specifically the format that such proposals must take, sometimes right down to the headings to be used. When such is the case, follow the instructions given in the RFP point by point. Not to do so will likely result in a rejected proposal.

In an unsolicited proposal, an organization sees a problem that another organization has and offers to provide the solution through its services. The following section describes a format that could be used in an unsolicited proposal, and the section following that describes a format that a student could use to propose a project to a teacher.

Unsolicited Proposals

Short proposals may look like correspondence. Longer proposals may need title pages, tables of contents, and so forth (all described in Chapter 8, Elements of Reports). In either case, the central format of the proposal will look something like this:

Project summary
Project description
    Introduction
    Rationale and significance
    Plan of work
    Facilities and equipment
Personnel
Budget
Appendixes

A *project summary* is essentially an executive summary (see pp. 88–91). In it, you briefly summarize your proposed services and emphasize the objectives of your proposal. Be sure to highlight how meeting those objectives will satisfy the needs of the client organization.

A *project description* comprises six sections: (1) introduction, (2) rationale and significance, (3) plan of work, (4) facilities and equipment, (5) personnel, and (6) budget.

1. Be sure your *introduction* (see pp. 92–94) makes clear the services you are proposing and how the successful outcome of your proposal will benefit your proposed client.

2. In *Rationale and Significance,* define the problem and make clear the need for a solution, describe the solution, show that the solution is feasible, and give the benefits of the solution. This section has the characteristics of an analytical report (see pp. 112–18).

3.   To carry out your solution, you must have a *plan of work*. A plan of work section comprises smaller elements that state your scope, describe your methodology, break your work into its component tasks, and schedule your work:

- Describe the scope of the work to be done; that is, make clear what you will do and, sometimes, what you will not do. Being careful about describing scope may prevent later difficulties with clients who expect work that they think you have promised.
- Describe your methodology. For example, will your research define the problem you perceive in the organization? If so, what methods will you use? Will you, perhaps, use focus groups and questionnaires? If so, how will you evaluate the results you get through these methods? Show your potential clients you know what you're doing.
- The proposed work can no doubt be broken down into smaller tasks. For example, you may first give a test questionnaire to a small group. After evaluating the results, you may modify the questionnaire and give it to all the client's employees. Next, you may evaluate the results, and so on.

When you have made your work plan and its component tasks clear, give your schedule for completion of that plan. You may find a flowchart (see pp. 57–59), showing your tasks in relation to the time it will take to accomplish them, useful for clarifying your schedule.

4.   In the *facilities and equipment* section, tell your prospective clients what facilities and equipment you will need and how you plan to get access to them. Answer questions like these: If you need a certain kind of laboratory, do you already have use of it? Do you have the equipment needed? If not, how do you plan to get it? Who will pay for it, you or the client? If the client will pay, will you use this equipment exclusively for the client? If not, how big a share must the client pay? You have a legal as well as an ethical responsibility to state clearly the answers to such questions.

5.   In the *personnel* section, list the people who will work on the project, if the proposal is accepted. Give details of their relevant educa-

tion and experience, such as the dates of past projects of a similar nature, the names and addresses of previous clients, and publications in
the field of the proposal. The more detailed you can be about relevant
qualifications, the better the chance of your proposal being accepted.

6.   Finally, you present your *budget.* In a table or list of some sort,
itemize your costs. If you have an extensive budget, you may need a classification scheme—for example, equipment, laboratory costs, salaries,
travel, fee, and so forth.

In addition to these six sections, you may need *appendixes* to your
project description (see p. 97). Appendixes may include additional budget information, biographical information, company background, histories of earlier successful projects, and so forth. In making your selection, remember that your proposal is a sales document that is being read
by busy people. They will read relevant appendixes but be put off by
anything that looks too much like boilerplate.

Student Proposals

Students frequently must propose projects of various sorts to their
teachers. For instance, a student in an advanced biology class may have
to propose an experiment that runs over the semester. A student in a
writing class may have to propose a project such as a feasibility report. If
you are a student and a teacher gives you a plan for the proposal, follow
it carefully. In the absence of such instructions, a scaled-down version of
the unsolicited proposal will be appropriate. The following is an accepted format:

- Combined executive summary (see pp. 88–91) and introduction
  (see pp. 92–94) that makes clear the subject, purpose, scope, and
  benefits of the project
- Task and time schedule
- Resources needed and where they are available
- Your qualifications for carrying out the project

(See Appendix B for a sample student proposal.)

Progress Reports

If you are working for a client, he or she has a natural interest in the answer to the question: How are you doing? Progress reports are designed to answer that question. Some work, particularly work that results from an accepted proposal, requires progress reports at stated intervals, perhaps monthly. Whether written to schedule or at irregular intervals, progress reports follow fairly standard formats.

What follows is one such format. Like all reports, if it is only a few pages long, write the progress report as a memo or letter. If it is long and involved, add title pages and the like, as needed.

Introduction

Use a standard introduction (see pp. 92–94). Make clear what work you are reporting.

Project Description

In a project description, briefly describe the work being done, being sure to clearly state its purpose and scope. The scope statement breaks the work down into its component tasks—for example, devise questionnaires, administer questionnaires, evaluate questionnaire results, write final report.

Work Completed

Tell the reader what you have accomplished to date. In a long-running project, requiring several progress reports covering several periods, you might divide this section further as follows:

> Summary of work accomplished in preceding periods
> Work accomplished in reporting period

You may further subdivide these sections by the tasks you have indicated in your scope statement, like this:

> Work accomplished in reporting period:
>> Devising questionnaires
>> Administering questionnaires
>> Evaluating questionnaires
>> Writing final report

Work Planned for Future Periods
Work planned for next period
Work planned for future periods

Appraisal of Progress
Evaluate your progress. Indicate where you are ahead of plan and where you are behind. Don't offer a litany of excuses, but if there are good reasons as to why the work is not going to plan, state them clearly. The executive summary (see pp. 88–91) is a good model for this appraisal.

As in all writing, don't complicate your progress reports any more than necessary, but do answer thoroughly a client's three basic questions:

1. What have you done?
2. What are you going to do next?
3. How are you doing?

(See Appendix C for a sample progress report.)

Empirical Research Reports

If you pursue a scientific career, you will frequently have to report the results of your empirical research. The format of an empirical research report closely parallels the stages of the scientific method. Scientists typically start with questions for which they want answers. They then review the literature to see if other scientists have asked the same or similar questions. If the specific questions have not been answered, the scientists devise methods to get at the answers, often by revising previously reported research. When the results of the research are in, scientists analyze them in the light of previous research to see what they mean and to arrive at conclusions. Because the overall format of the research report follows their research patterns so well, scientists find it easier to organize their research reports than they otherwise might. The major components of an empirical research reports are as follows:

Abstract
Introduction
Literature Review
Materials and Methods
Results
Discussion
Conclusions

Abstract

The abstract summarizes key points of the report, including objectives of the research, major results, and conclusions. After reading it, the reader will know the objective of the research, why the research was conducted, the major results, the meaning of the results, and the major conclusions of the author. The reader now has many options: Read the entire report, read only the discussion to see how the author analyzes the results, check out the conclusions, and so forth. The reader's knowledge, needs, and interests, not the author's, govern the options chosen.

Introduction

The introduction describes the subject, scope, significance, and objectives of the research.

Literature Review

The literature review summarizes previous research that has bearing on the research being reported. Such research may address objectives, materials and methods, and the rationale for the work done. To learn and understand, readers have to be led from the known to the unknown— that which is to be learned. Most formats allow for this logical progression. In the case of the empirical research report, the introduction and literature review together serve this purpose. By reviewing past research in the field, the literature review provides the necessary background to understand the objective of the research, the need for the research, and the techniques used in the research.

With this new knowledge, the reader can follow the descriptions of the materials and methods used in the research. With materials and methods understood, the reader can comprehend the results they achieved. With all the preceding known, the reader can follow the analysis of the results and understand the conclusions.

The progression from the known to the unknown also supports selective reading. For instance, the reader may already know the background and techniques of the immediate research well. Such knowledge allows the reader to move directly to the results and discussion.

In journal articles, the literature review is most often integrated with the introduction. In dissertations, the literature review usually stands by itself with its own heading.

Materials and Methods

The materials and methods section may describe any of the following: the design of the research, the materials used, the procedures followed, or the methods for observation and evaluation. An experienced researcher in the field should be able to replicate the research using this section as a guide.

Results

The results section is a factual accounting of what the researcher has found. Writers of research reports make extensive use of tables and graphs in the results section.

Discussion

The discussion section is an analytical discussion that interprets the results (see pp. 112–18). It answers questions such as these: Were the research objectives met? If not, why not? How well do the results correlate with results from previous research? If they do not correlate well, why not? What future work should follow this research? In many formats, the results and discussion are combined.

Conclusions

If the researcher's conclusions are not integrated into the discussion, they are stated here.

(See Appendix D for a sample empirical research report. You should also carefully study the reports published in the journals that cover your field of study.)

10

Formats of Correspondence

Letters are used for correspondence outside an organization. *Memorandums* (or *memos*) are used for correspondence within an organization.

Letters and memos may (and in some cases should) contain many of the elements found in more formal reports (as described in Chapter 8, Elements of Reports). That is, they may contain introductions, summaries (particularly executive summaries), discussions, conclusions, and recommendations. However, these elements may be somewhat abbreviated. They also may be labeled differently—"Findings" or "Discussion," for instance—or have substantive headings, such as "Existing Patient Populations." Such labeling is particularly appropriate for letters and memos that substitute for longer, more formal reports. (See Appendix A for an example of a letter report.)

Shorter letters and memos that convey information or opinions, make complaints, answer complaints, and so forth may have simple introductions and perhaps even summaries but will not label them as such.

The first section of this chapter deals with the formal elements used in standard letters. The second, third, and fourth sections deal with some important stylistic elements in simplified letters, memos, and e-mail. The closing section describes the correspondence used in a job hunt: résumés and letters of application.

Formal Elements of Letters

One of the disadvantages of having a personal computer on every desk is that executives in middle-management ranks are sometimes responsible for producing their own correspondence. Therefore, the formal elements of correspondence may be more important to you than you would like to believe. Also, good page design (see Chapter 5) is as important in letters as in reports.

Both Appendix A and Figure 10.1 illustrate well-formatted business letters. The following sections explain the components found in such letters.

Letterhead

On the job, you will likely have a printed letterhead on your stationery, containing your organization's address, telephone and fax numbers, and the like. Figure 10.1 shows a typical printed letterhead. If you don't have a printed letterhead, as might be the case when you are job hunting, simply place your address flush left, as illustrated in Figure 10.8 (p. 145).

Notice in the figures that standard postal abbreviations are used for states and provinces (see Figure 10.2, p. 131). However, words such as *Street, Road,* and so forth are not abbreviated.

Date Line

Use one of these two styles for date lines: *16 March 2000* or *March 16, 2000.* Notice that the month is not abbreviated and number suffixes, such as *th* and *nd,* are not used.

Inside Address

Place the name and address of the person receiving the letter four spaces below the date line. Use a courtesy title, such as *Ms.* or *Professor,* with the name. The abbreviations *Mr., Ms.,* and *Dr.* are standard usage. Other

B R O W E R C O N S T R U C T I O N C O M P A N Y
1998 Lee Highway
Freedom, MO 63032
Phone: 314-555-6788
Fax: 314-555-3097

July 27, 2000

Mrs. Irma Weaver
2 Brightside Lane
Freedom, MO 63032

Re: Your letter of July 17, 1996

Subject: Proposed solution of underground tank problem

Dear Mrs. Weaver:

We regret the installation of the underground oil tank on your
property when we built your house. We did, indeed, receive
the notice from the town clerk about the new city ordinance
prohibiting underground oil tanks for environmental reasons.
Unfortunately, for some reason, the news about the ordinance
did not reach our design team in time.

However, the town clerk tells us that during the winter everyone
with a building permit received a notice of the new ordinance.
Your permit number was 615002. Apparently, you overlooked
the notice, as did we.

(continued)

FIGURE 10.1 Standard Business Letter

Page 2
Mrs. Irma Weaver
27 July 2000

I think we have a shared responsibility in this matter, and neither of us should bear the full cost. Let me suggest the following: We will remove the underground tank and fittings, close off and seal the opening in your foundation, and fill the hole at no labor or material cost to you. We will charge you labor costs for installing an indoor tank and the difference between the price of the outside tank and the new indoor tank. Your total cost will be $420.34.

If this arrangement is satisfactory to you, please call and we'll schedule the work. We regret any inconvenience you and Mr. Weaver have experienced and hope you will continue to enjoy your new house.

Sincerely yours,

Howard Brower

Howard Brower
Chief Operating Officer

HB: pgc

Encl. Copy of town clerk's letter to building permit holders

FIGURE 10.1   **Continued**

courtesy titles, such as *Professor* and *Captain,* are spelled out. When you use the courtesy title *Dr.* before the name, do not use the equivalent (for example, *Ph.D.*) after the name. Put a one-word job title, such as *Director,* after the name. Place a job title of two or more words on the next line after the name.

United States				*Canada*	
Alabama	AL	Missouri	MO	Alberta	AB
Alaska	AK	Montana	MT	British Columbia	BC
American		Nebraska	NE	Labrador	LB
Samoa	AS	Nevada	NV	Manitoba	MB
Arizona	AZ	New Hampshire	NH	New Brunswick	NB
Arkansas	AR	New Jersey	NJ	Newfoundland	NF
California	CA	New Mexico	NM	Nova Scotia	NS
Colorado	CO	New York	NY	Northwest	
Connecticut	CT	North Carolina	NC	Territories	NT
Delaware	DE	North Dakota	ND	Ontario	ON
District of		Ohio	OH	Prince Edward	
Columbia	DC	Oklahoma	OK	Island	PE
Florida	FL	Oregon	OR	Quebec (Province	
Georgia	GA	Pennsylvania	PA	de Quebec)	PQ
Guam	GU	Puerto Rico	PR	Saskatchewan	SK
Hawaii	HI	Rhode Island	RI	Yukon Territory	YT
Idaho	ID	South Carolina	SC		
Illinois	IL	South Dakota	SD		
Indiana	IN	Tennessee	TN		
Iowa	IA	Texas	TX		
Kansas	KS	Utah	UT		
Kentucky	KY	Vermont	VT		
Louisiana	LA	Virginia	VA		
Maine	ME	Virgin Islands	VI		
Maryland	MD	Washington	WA		
Massachusetts	MA	West Virginia	WV		
Michigan	MI	Wisconsin	WI		
Minnesota	MN	Wyoming	WY		
Mississippi	MS				

FIGURE 10.2   State, Territory, and Province Abbreviations for the United States and Canada

As in the letterhead, abbreviate names of states and provinces but not words like *Street*. Write the names of organizations and people exactly as they do. Use *Inc.*, not *Incorporated*, if the company does. Use *F. Xavier Jones*, not *Frank X. Jones*, if he does.

Re *Line*

The *Re* in the *re* line stands for "reference." Generally, the reference is to other documents, as in *Your letter of 12 April 2000* or *Your contract with Smith Brothers, dated 16 May 2000*.

Subject Line

In a subject line, you tell the reader what subject will be dealt with in your letter—for example, *Summer Schedule for Executive Committee Meetings*. Sometimes, the word *Subject* is used in the subject line, as in Figure 10.1. When *Subject* is omitted, the subject line is generally all capital letters, as in Figure 10.3 (p. 135).

Salutation

For the most part, we still adhere to tradition and begin salutations with *Dear*. Follow *Dear* with the name used in the inside address—*Dear Ms. Pleasant* and so forth. Use a colon after the salutation, and place it as shown in Figure 10.1.

If you do not have a name to use, you have one of two choices: If it's an important letter—a proposal, for instance—get a name, even if it takes a long-distance phone call to do so. If it's a routine letter—such as an inquiry—use a simplified letter, as shown in Figure 10.3.

Body

Keep body paragraphs short, rarely more than six or seven lines, and space them as indicated in Figures 10.1 and 10.2. Do not split words between lines. Also do not split dates or names; that is, *February 11, 2000* should be on one line, as should be *Margaret M. Briand*.

Complimentary Close

In most business correspondence, use a simple complimentary close, such as *Sincerely yours.* In instances in which friendships are involved, closes such as *Best regards* are suitable. Follow the close with a comma, and place it as in Figure 10.1.

Signature Block

Four spaces below the complimentary close, type your name and, if you have one, your title. To avoid complicating the life of a correspondent who doesn't know you, use enough of your name to indicate your gender. That is, use *Patrick M. Fields,* not *Pat Fields* or *P. M. Fields.* In the space between the complimentary close and your typed name, sign your name—legibly, please.

End Notations

Notations following the signature block indicate such things as identification, enclosures, and copies (see Figure 10.1).

Identification
In this type of notation, the writer's initials are in capital letters and the secretary's initials are in lowercase:

FDR/hrc

Enclosures
Enclosure lines indicate to the reader—sometimes in a general way, sometimes specifically—that you have enclosed additional material with your letter, as in the following two examples:

Enclosures (3)

Encl: Schedule for summer meetings

Copy
In a copy line, you tell your correspondent who is receiving a copy of the letter:

cc. Dr. Georgia Brown

Mr. Hugh Binns

Continuation Page

When your letter exceeds one page, you need a continuation page or pages (see Figure 10.1). Follow these rules when constructing a continuation page:

- Use paper of the same color and weight as your first page, but do not use letterhead stationery.
- As in Figure 10.1, head the continuation page with the page number, the name of your correspondent, and the date.
- Have at least three lines of text on the last continuation page before the complimentary close and whatever else follows.
- The last paragraph on the page that precedes the last continuation page should contain at least two lines.

Simplified Letters

The simplified letter (see Figure 10.3), as its name implies, is a simplified form of the standard letter. It always has a subject line, but it does not have either a salutation or a complimentary close. In every other respect, it follows the format of a standard letter.

Use a simplified letter for routine correspondence only when you do not have the name of a person to address. You could use it, for example, to register a complaint with an organization or to make a simple inquiry to some department within an organization. Do not use a simplified letter to answer complaints (where good strategy calls for you to address the person complaining by name) or for important letters like letter reports.

Memorandums

Memorandums are used for correspondence within an organization. They most often are written on printed forms that are headed with the organization's name and spaces for *date, to, from,* and *subject* (see Figure 10.4). Because of the memo's format, a salutation and signature block are not needed. The body of a memo and its continuation page look

BROWER CONSTRUCTION COMPANY

1998 Lee Highway
Freedom, MO 63032
Phone: 314-555-6788
Fax: 314-555-3097

26 March 2000

Director, Corporate Research and Engineering
Burnham, Inc.
3660 Folwell Drive
Minneapolis, MN 55418

SPREAD-SPECTRUM HOME SECURITY SYSTEMS

Our company installs a good many Burnham Home Security Systems
in the new homes we construct. These systems are hard wired, which
presents no problems in new construction. However, increasingly,
we are asked to provide security systems in existing homes. Here,
hard wiring presents problems for which the only solution is running
wires through walls, with all the accompanying expense.

I understand that Burnham is working on wireless security systems
using a spread-spectrum modulation technique that will allow radiofrequency communication between the components of a home
security system.

How far along is your research on this new system? Do you have a
target date for marketing it? When it is ready, we will certainly
consider it for use in both new construction and existing homes.

Howard Brower

Howard Brower
Chief Operating Officer

HB: pgc

FIGURE 10.3   Simplified Letter

precisely like the body and continuation page of a letter. A memo also uses the same end notations as a letter.

Memos may be used for any of the purposes for which letters are used. That is, you can write memos that provide information or make inquiries or memo reports that, like letter reports, are short reports containing summaries, introductions, headings, and so forth.

E-mail

The speed and simplicity of e-mail have led to its widespread use both within and without organizations. In many instances, it has replaced telephone calls and short memos and letters. E-mail format is determined by the online organization used, but most formats include blanks similar to memo entries for address, subject, message, and so forth (see Figure 10.4).

The messages sent by e-mail tend to be brief. When used among trusted colleagues, e-mail messages are likely to be highly informal and full of abbreviations and other shortcuts, perhaps known only to those sending and receiving them. However, when sending e-mail to authority figures or people you don't know well, be more circumspect.

If you do not save the e-mail messages you send and receive, you may face the same pitfall as with phone conversations: That is, people's memories of what was actually said or implied may differ widely.

E-mail is probably best used for sending needed information and opinions but not for the equivalent of letter or memo reports.

Correspondence of the Job Search

Begin your job-search correspondence by brainstorming the elements of your past education and job experience. With the help of college transcripts, memory, and any journals and records you had the foresight to keep, list details such as dates, job titles, course titles, professors' and employers' names, work accomplished, and so forth. Make your list as extensive as possible. The information you record will furnish material for résumés and letters of application, the two most important pieces of correspondence of the job search.

Memo Format

Roswell Electric

Date: 12 February 1999

To: Tom Hovey
              Vice President

From: Barbara Gamez   *BG*
              Plant Engineer

Subject: Improving Plant Power Consumption

An article in the January 1999 *Mechanical Engineering* (pp. 62–63) describes how TU Electric was able to reduce their plant's pumping power consumption significantly. Encor-American Technologies, Inc., conducted field observations and computer simulated flow studies that revealed turbulence in TU's system was wasting power. Implementing changes recommended by Encor reduced TU's power consumption by 9%.

I recommend that we contact Encor and request a consultation.

E-mail Format

To: thovey@Ru.org

Subject: Improving plant power consumption

Tom, an article in the January 1999 <u>Mechanical Engineering</u> (pp. 62-63) describes how TU Electric was able to reduce their plant's pumping power consumption significantly. Encor-American Technologies, Inc., conducted field observations and computer simulated flow studies that revealed turbulence in TU's system was wasting power. Implementing changes recommended by Encor reduced TU's power consumption by 9%. I think we should contact Encor and request a consultation. Barbara G.

FIGURE 10.4   Message in Memo and E-Mail Formats

Résumés

A *résumé* is the summary of your education and job experience that you send to potential employers. From it and the accompanying letter of application, potential employers will decide whether to interview you. Thus, your résumé is a very important document. See Figures 10.5, 10.6, and 10.7 for example résumés (pp. 139, 141, and 143, respectively).

The two most widely used kinds of résumés are the *chronological* and the *functional*. Both can be done in a standard paper format or in digital formats suitable for e-mailing or scanning.

Chronological Résumés

Look at Figure 10.5. Begin a chronological resume with your name and address and list all the ways you can be reached: mail, phone, fax, and e-mail. Next, give the details of your higher education: school or schools attended, degree, expected graduation date, major, minor, course work, extracurricular activities, and so forth. Avoid the constant use of *I* by using fragmentary sentences.

You should indicate your academic standing in the most favorable way you legitimately can. If your GPA in your major is higher than your overall GPA, use that. If your record is really bad, don't list it. If you attended more than one college, list the last one first and so on.

Give the details of your work experience. As with your education, do it in reverse chronological order. Don't merely list job titles. Using action verbs like *managed, operated, organized, sold,* and *designed,* describe what you did. List all the jobs of your college years, even those that don't relate to the jobs you are seeking. Employers feel, quite correctly, that people who have worked understand the workplace better than those who have not.

If you have room, give a few details of your personal background. Sometimes, employers will see something there that interests them, particularly people skills, which they value highly.

Offer to supply references. Use both professors and employers (more on this later). Finish off with the month and year of the résumé.

The advantage of the chronological resume is that it provides a smooth summary, year by year, of your education and experience. If growth is there, this type of résumé will show it well. But if your education and experience have big gaps, the chronological résumé may not be

RÉSUMÉ OF JANICE OSBORN

32 Merchant Road
St. Paul, MN 55101
Phone: (612) 555-6755
E-Mail: josborn@wave.com

Education **1996-2000**	**University of Minnesota, St. Paul, MN** Candidate for Bachelor of Science degree in Technical Communication with a minor in Computer Science in June 2000. In upper third of class with a GPA of 3.0 on a 4.0 scale. Member of St. Paul Student Council, vice president in senior year. Served as editorial assistant, 1998-2000 for *Technical Communication Quarterly*, the journal of the Association of Teachers of Technical Writing. Corresponded with authors and copyedited articles.
Business **Experience** **1999** **Summer**	**Communication Design Associates,** **Minneapolis, MN** As part of five-person team, assisted large corporation in using SGML (Standard Generalized Markup Language) to convert 10,000 pages of paper documentation to online documentation.
1997-1998 **Summers**	**Technical Publications, Inc.** Using desktop publishing techniques, worked collaboratively and individually in developing manuals, proposals, and feasibility reports.
Personal **Background**	Grew up in International Falls, Minnesota. Have traveled in United States and France. Enjoy music, Alpine and Nordic skiing, and browsing Internet.
References	References available on request.

March 2000

FIGURE 10.5 Chronological Résumé

the better choice. Also, your skills and aptitudes may tend to get lost in the welter of dates, courses, and jobs. Despite all that, the chronological résumé is a good format.

Functional Résumés

Look at Figure 10.6. Begin a functional résumé with your name, address, phone number, and the like, as in the chronological résumé. Next, give your degree, major and minor, and expected graduation date. If you attended more than one college, give them in reverse chronological order.

The heart of a functional résumé is a classification of your experiences—academic, extracurricular, and work—that demonstrates your skills and capabilities. (See pp. 17–18 for the rules of classification.) Using category words such as *professional, technical, people, communication, management, marketing, sales,* and *research,* create two or three categories that show you off the best.

Finish the résumé with a reverse chronological listing of your jobs, an offer of references, and the date.

The advantage of the functional résumé is that it brings to the fore your skills and capabilities. There is a slight disadvantage in that it does not show the smooth progression of the chronological résumé. Choose the résumé that displays you to your best advantage.

Résumé Formats

You have several options for delivering your résumé. If you are going to mail it through the postal service, you may use a standard format. However, if you know the employer is going to scan your résumé into a database, use a scannable digital format. If you are requested to send it via e-mail, also use a digital format.

Standard Format.   In the standard format, you can take advantage of the font possibilities on a word processor, but use discretion and good page design (see Chapter 5). Don't fill your résumé with exotic typefaces. The mix of plain print and boldface in Figures 10.5 and 10.6 illustrates the look you want.

RÉSUMÉ OF JANICE OSBORN

32 Merchant Road
St. Paul, MN 55101
Phone: (612) 555-6755
E-Mail: josborn@wave.com

Education	Candidate for Bachelor of Science degree in Technical Communication with a minor in Computer Science from University of Minnesota in June 2000.

Professional
- Working under pressure, used desktop publishing to produce high-quality manuals, proposals, and feasibility reports.
- As part of five-person team, assisted large corporation in using SGML (Standard Generalized Markup Language) to convert 10,000 pages of paper documentation to online documentation.
- Assisted editor of professional journal in copyediting manuscripts and corresponding with authors.
- Completed courses in writing, editing, speaking, desktop publishing, graphics, management, multimedia, and computer science.

People
- Elected vice president of St. Paul Campus Student Council. Oversaw student recreational budget.
- Successfully worked in collaboration with other writers and editors.
- Know how to accept criticism and use it constructively.

Work Experience

1999 Summer
- Communication Design Associates, Minneapolis, MN: Writer and member of consulting team.

1995–2000
- *Technical Communication Quarterly*, St. Paul Campus: Editorial Assistant.

1997, 1998 Summers
- Technical Publications, Minneapolis, MN: Technical writer and editor.

References   References available on request.

March 2000

FIGURE 10.6   Functional Résumé

Résumés in any format must be mechanically perfect—no misspellings, typos, or grammatical errors. If you need help to accomplish this, get help.

When finished, print your résumé on good-quality white paper using a letter-quality printer. Never fold or staple your résumé.

Digital Format. Figure 10.7 illustrates a digital résumé. Use a digital format to e-mail a résumé or when you know the potential employer will scan your résumé into a database. If uncertain as to whether an employer will want a scannable copy, send both standard and scannable résumés.

To ensure that your digital résumé can be read, you must use plain text. *Plain text,* absent any special formatting codes, can be read by any computer or scanner. Follow these guidelines in constructing your digital résumé:

- Do not use boldface, italics, underlining, or any of the other design features available on a word processor.
- Use single columns, aligned at the left, with no more than 65 characters a line.
- Use a standard-width typeface—for example, `Courier`.
- Use capital letters when you want emphasis.
- Space with the space bar, not tabs.

When managers want to pull up résumés from a database, they will look for *key words* that match terms used in the field in which the jobs are located. Look for key words in job announcements for your field, and include them in your résumé.

If you e-mail your résumé, include your letter of application, constructed in a digital format, as part of your message. *Do not* send your letter of application as an attachment to your résumé. People may not be able to open the attachment or, fearing a virus, will not open it. If you mail your scannable digital résumé through the postal service, print it and the accompanying letter of application on good-quality white paper. Do not fold or staple either one.

RÉSUMÉ OF JANICE OSBORN

32 Merchant Road
St. Paul, MN 55101
Phone: (612) 555-6755
E-Mail: josborn@wave.com

EDUCATION
University of Minnesota, St. Paul, MN, 1996-2000
Candidate for Bachelor of Science degree in Technical
Communication with a minor in Computer Science in June 2000.
In upper third of class with a GPA of 3.0 on a 4.0 scale.

Member of St. Paul Student Council, vice president in senior year.
Served as editorial assistant, 1994-1996 for Technical
Communication Quarterly, the Journal of the Association of
Teachers of Technical Writing. Corresponded with authors and
copyedited articles.

BUSINESS EXPERIENCE
Communication Design Associates
Minneapolis, MN, Summer 1999

As part of five-person team, assisted large corporation in using
SGML (Standard Generalized Markup Language) to convert
10,000 pages of paper documentation to online documentation.

Technical Publications, Inc.
St. Paul, MN, Summers 1997, 1998
Using desktop publishing techniques, worked
collaboratively and individually in developing manuals,
proposals, and feasibility reports.

PERSONAL INFORMATION
Grew up in International Falls, Minnesota. Have traveled in
United States and France. Enjoy music, Alpine and Nordic skiing,
and browsing Internet.

REFERENCES
Available on request.

March 2000

FIGURE 10.7   Digital Résumé

Letters of Application

When you send out your résumé, accompany it with a letter of application (see Figure 10.8). The letter of application is a letter of transmittal for the résumé, but it is also a place where you can highlight your capabilities and catch an employer's interest. If you are discreet about it, you can use your letter of application to point out how you could fit into the organization and why it would be to the employer's advantage to hire you. Blow your own horn but not directly in the employer's ear.

If possible, send your letter and résumé to the person for whom you might work. A potential supervisor is better able to judge your qualifications than a human resources officer. Often, a letter or phone call to the organization might get you the name you need. Looking through professional journals in your field will often provide such names as will networking with professionals. Websites and forums on the Internet also provide useful information about employers. Send letters and résumés to human resources divisions if need be but only as a last resort.

A good way to start your letter is by dropping a name known to the potential employer. However, do this only with permission. Indicate some knowledge of the organization, which you can gather in the same way as names. In the middle of the letter, *sell yourself*. Use specific education and work experiences to point out your potential value and usefulness to the organization.

In the close of the letter, refer to your résumé and references. If you have significant products from your work or education (such as research reports, manuals, videos, and so forth), offer to send them. Finally, try to arrange an interview. Make it as convenient for the employer as you possibly can.

Other Correspondence

Several other pieces of correspondence are necessary during the job search, none of them difficult or time consuming to do.

When you ask your references for permission to use their names, provide them with copies of your résumé. If you can, call on them. If you can't, write each person a letter, recalling your relationship with him or her and asking for his or her permission.

Sending several thank-you notes is appropriate during and after the job search. When you interview, get the interviewer's name and address; later, write a note, expressing appreciation for the interview. When your

32 Merchant Road
St. Paul, MN 55101
(612) 555-6755
josborn@wave.com

9 March 2000

Mr. James Cantrell
Supervisor of Writing and Publications
Bell Computer Corporation
4200 Lake Avenue
Madison, WI 53714

Dear Mr. Cantrell:

Professor Robert Wilson of the University of Minnesota Computer
Science Department tells me that your firm designs communication
protocols that allow two or more computer networks to operate as
one network. This is a field of great interest to me, and I think I have
the education and experience to serve Bell Computer well.

In June, I will graduate from the University's Technical
Communication program with a minor in Computer Science. I have
completed courses in writing, editing, speaking, desktop publishing,
graphics, management, multimedia, and computer science.

In the summers of 1997 and 1998, I worked as a technical writer and
editor using desktop publishing to produce high-quality manuals,
proposals, and feasibility reports. Last summer, I worked on a team
helping a large corporation use SGML to convert paper files into
online files. This experience, combined with my education, would
allow me to fit into your operation quickly.

The enclosed résumé gives more detailed information about my
education and experience. I can provide references from both
my teachers and employers.

May I come to Madison to discuss job opportunities with you? If
that is not convenient, I'll be attending the International Technical
Communication Conference in May. Perhaps we can talk there.

Sincerely yours,

Janice Osborn

Janice Osborn

Janice Osborn

FIGURE 10.8   Letter of Application

job search succeeds, write thank-you notes to all your references. Give them the outcome of the search, and thank them for their help. They'll be curious about the result and pleased with your thoughtfulness.

If you are offered jobs at several organizations, drop a note of thanks and refusal to each of the organizations you turn down. Simply express your appreciation for the job offer, thank them for their time and interest, and perhaps compliment them on their organization.

Further Information

For additional information, go to http://stats.bls.gov/opbhome.htm, a Bureau of Labor website. There you will find such things as the *Occupational Outlook Handbook,* which describes in depth 250 occupations and provides useful information for the job search.

APPENDIXES

Sample Reports

APPENDIX A

Letter Analytical Report

Analytical reports up to six or seven pages long are likely to be written as correspondence, as is the report in this sample. The sample uses a problem-solution organization. In the interests of accessibility, selective reading, and comprehension, it contains a good introduction that makes clear the subject, purpose, and scope of the report. Headings also aid selective reading and display the report's organization. The Recommendation section makes good use of listing techniques.

Environmental Consultants
2063 Peach Tree Street
Suite 260
Atlanta, GA 30747
Phone: 404-555-1940
Fax: 404-555-9003
E-mail: nlarsen@enco.com

November 20, 2000

Mr. James Morris
Chief Executive Officer
Albany Office Products
22 Oglethorpe Road
Albany, GA 30278

Subject: Inspection Findings and Recommendations

Dear Mr. Morris:

As you engaged us to do, we have examined the environmental
problems in your company headquarters. This report provides
background for our report, states the problems our inspection
uncovered, and recommends solutions for them.

Background

For the last year, the workers in your two-story office building
have experienced higher-than-average health problems. They
have suffered from watery eyes, nasal congestion, coughing,
difficulty breathing, headache, and fatigue. Last winter, your

workers had a high incidence of flu, and lost work days grew to unacceptable levels because of it. During the last six months, three of your employees with asthma had to be hospitalized.

Although these problems were not limited to your first-floor offices, they were more prevalent there than on the second floor. All these reactions pointed to the presence of excessive biological pollution in your building, particularly on the first floor.

Biological pollutants are found everywhere. Molds, bacteria, and viruses are commonly found in office buildings such as yours. People exposed to such pollutants may suffer allergic reactions, infections, and even serious toxic reactions in the central nervous system and the immune system.

Biological pollutants need moisture to grow and spread. When moisture levels in a building are lowered, the level of pollutants and the reactions to them are greatly reduced. Therefore, our inspection of your building focused on moisture problems, particularly on the first floor.

Findings of the Inspection

Our inspection found major problems with your first-floor carpet and heating and air-conditioning ducts. We found also a minor problem with the large number of coffee makers in your building.

First-Floor Carpeting

Your building is slab constructed, and bare concrete underlies all of the matting and wall-to-wall carpet on the first floor. Moisture has passed through the concrete and allowed mold to grow and spread in and under the matting and the carpet. Spot inspections indicate that more than 80 percent of the first-floor carpet has mold growing underneath it. Where mold is found, you can be sure that bacteria and viruses also flourish. This condition most certainly explains the high incidence of health problems on the first floor.

Heating and Air-Conditioning Ducts

The heating and air-conditioning ducts are full of dust and are beginning to show signs of mold. The heater and air conditioner had not been properly cleaned, and the system filters were clogged with dust. These conditions explain the incidence of health problems on the second floor.

Coffee Makers

Office policy obviously does not regulate the use of coffee makers throughout the building. We found 18 coffee makers plugged in and working during our inspection. These coffee makers put a great deal of moisture into the air, encouraging the growth of pollutants.

Recommended Solutions

The problems encountered in your building all have ready solutions.

First-Floor Carpeting

The first-floor carpeting and matting are too far gone to be salvaged. They must be taken up and discarded. The concrete floor must be professionally cleaned and disinfected. Following that, you have two alternatives:

Page 4
Mr. James Morris
November 20, 2000

- Lay a plastic vapor barrier on the concrete and cover that
  with a subfloor of insulation and plywood. Matting and wall-
  to-wall carpet can then be laid on the plywood.

- A somewhat less expensive alternative would be to lay
  good-quality asphalt or vinyl tile on the concrete and use
  area rugs where carpeting is wanted.

Heating and Air-Conditioning Ducts

You need to take three steps to keep your heating and air-
conditioning ducts free of pollution:

- Have the heating and air-conditioning units and their ducts
  professionally cleaned as soon as possible but not until after
  the carpet problem has been resolved. (Removing the carpet,
  cleaning the concrete floor, and laying subflooring or tile will
  kick up dust and dirt.)

- Contract with heating and air-conditioning professionals to
  have them clean your heaters and air conditioners at the
  start of each heating and cooling period.

- Arrange to have your building cleaners change your system
  filters monthly.

Coffee Makers

Remove the coffee makers from the various offices. If you wish,
in some well-ventilated space, place one or two larger coffee
makers that everyone can use.

Page 5
Mr. James Morris
November 20, 2000

The recommended solutions follow the guidelines laid down by the U.S. Consumer Product Safety Commission and the American Lung Association. While air pollution cannot be completely eliminated, short of extraordinary measures, carrying out the work recommended will restore a healthful environment to your workplace.

If you want our assistance in locating the professionals to carry out the needed work, let us know. Thank you for letting us help you.

Sincerely,

Nancy Larsen

Nancy Larsen
Chief of Inspections

NL: siu

APPENDIX   B

Student Proposal

Although a *student* proposal, this sample provides much the same information that might be found in a full-scale proposal. The introduction makes clear the purpose and scope of the work to be done, its rationale, and its significance both to the professor's proposed research and to the student. The Time and Task Breakdown section shows the student's plan of work. The Resources Available section parallels the more full-scale Facilities and Equipment of a large proposal. The listing of the journals and Internet materials available shows that the student has done a preliminary study, always a good sign to the person expected to approve a proposal. The Qualifications section, like a Personnel section, gives details of the student's education and experience that qualify her for the work proposed. Only the Budget section of a full-scale proposal is missing (and not needed) in this proposal.

MEMORANDUM

Date   12 January 2000

To   Professor William Fuller, Chair
Department of Environmental Engineering
University of New Mexico

From   Samantha Pearson   *SP*

Subject   Proposal for an Independent Study

Professor Isabella Mendoza of Environmental Engineering (EnEng) is planning a proposal for a pilot project to cleanse soils polluted by contaminants such as diesel fuel and gasoline. Her objective is to test the efficiency and cost effectiveness of steam injection combined with radiofrequency heating to remove the contaminants.

Professor Mendoza is aware of pipe failures that have been experienced while using steam injection. I have volunteered to help her by researching the literature to find ways of avoiding such failures. Also, she has asked me to investigate possible funding sources for the project. Conducting the literature search and reporting its results should help Professor Mendoza plan her project and increase my own research and writing skills.

I request that I be allowed to use this literature search and the resulting literature review to fulfill the requirements for three hours of independent study in Environmental Engineering 4500. Professor Mendoza will guide me in the search and be the instructor of record for the independent study.

Page 2
Professor Fuller
12 January 2000

Task and Time Breakdown
In order to be useful to Professor's Mendoza's planning,
the literature review should be in her hands by early April.
Therefore, I plan the following timetable:

1. Search the Internet and the periodicals and books in the
   university library for literature relevant to Professor
   Mendoza's concerns. Take notes on useful information.
   (4 weeks)

2. Prepare and submit a progress report on my search to
   Professor Mendoza, with a copy to you. (1 week)

3. Continue the search, and begin preliminary organization
   and analysis of the information gathered. (2 weeks)

4. Write a preliminary draft of the literature review, and
   submit it to Professor Mendoza, with a copy to you.
   Discuss the preliminary draft with Professor Mendoza.
   (2 weeks)

5. Write the final draft of the literature review, and submit
   it to Professor Mendoza, with a copy to you, no later than
   5 April.

Resources Available
The university's periodical collection in the area of the search
is comprehensive. The following periodicals seem particularly
relevant: *Environmental Science Technology, J. of Air Waste
Management Association, J. of Soil Contamination, J. of
Canadian Petroleum Technology, J. of Petroleum Technology,
J. of Soil Contamination,* and *Petroleum Engineering.*

Page 3
Professor Fuller
12 January 2000

Additionally, the library has large holdings of proceedings, reports, and books that seem pertinent. Finally, a preliminary exploration of websites reveals a good deal of material in the area. The Environmental Protection Agency has a wealth of information on the Internet concerning methodology and funding for cleaning contaminated sites.

Qualifications
As a senior student in an EnEng major, I have conducted numerous library and Internet searches. I have been a part-time employee in the EnEng laboratory for three semesters and understand the methodology and objectives of research. I successfully completed a three-hour independent study last year with Professor John Januzzo. My EnEng GPA is 3.8.

Progress Report

This progress report is the one called for by the proposal in Appendix B. Like all good progress reports, it answers the three questions every client wants answered: What have you done? What are you going to do next? How are you doing? The introduction and Project Description remind the client of what the subject and purpose of the research are. Under Work Completed, the writer provides enough detail to reassure the client that work is going well. The writer's dividing the Work Completed into two sections suggests what the organization of the proposed literature review will likely be. The Work Remaining section promises that the literature review will be done on time, and the Overall Appraisal encourages the client to believe that it will be useful.

MEMORANDUM

Date   24 February 2000

To   Professor Isabella Mendoza
Department of Environmental Engineering

From   Samantha Pearson *SP*

Subject   Progress Report on Independent Study
for EnEng 4500

I began work on this independent study on 20 January, after you and Professor Fuller accepted my proposal. This is the progress report scheduled in the proposal. It describes the work completed and the work remaining in the study and concludes with an appraisal of the progress of the study.

Project Description
The purpose of this independent study is to review literature pertinent to your planned proposal for a pilot project to cleanse soils polluted by such contaminants as diesel fuel and gasoline. The review includes four major tasks:

- Search for literature concerning the causes and solutions for pipe failures during steam injection.
- Search for funding sources for the pilot project.
- Organize and analyze the information gathered.
- Write a literature review based on the information gathered.

Page 2
Professor Mendoza
24 February 2000

Work Completed

During this reporting period, I focused on the first two tasks: finding information concerning pipe failures and funding. I found excellent information in both areas. Here, I will briefly outline what I have found:

Pipe Failures

A key article in my search for information on pipe failures was Eva L. Davis's "Steam Injection for Soil and Aquifer Remediation," in EPA's *Ground Water Issue,* January 1998. Davis points out that steam injection is a technology first used to recover oil from depleted oil fields that has been adapted for use in cleansing polluted soils. The problem of pipe failures was known to petroleum engineers and their solutions are still pertinent. Davis's article led me to several other excellent sources:

C. F. Gates and B. B. Holmes, *Thermal Well Completions and Operation,* Seventh World Petroleum Congress Proceedings 3 (1967): 419–29.

S. M. Ali Farouq and R. F. Maldau, "Current Steam Flood Technology," *J. Petroleum Technology* October 1979: 1332–42.

M. M. Schumacher, *Enhanced Recovery of Residual and Heavy Oils,* 2nd ed. (Park Ridge, NJ: Noyes Data Corporation, 1980).

C. Chu, "State of the Art Review of Steamflood Field Projects," *J. Petroleum Technology* October 1985: 1887–1902.

These sources recommend steel casing over PVC or fiberglass because of the extreme expansion and contraction that goes on during steam injection. They also provide mixture formulas for cement that will hold up under these extreme conditions.

Page 3
Professor Mendoza
24 February 2000

Funding
Numerous agencies provide funding for polluted site
remediation, but not all are interested in funding test or pilot
programs. I have listed some of those who do fund such
programs:

- National Environmental Technology Test Site Program, a
  partnership of the Environmental Protection Agency (EPA)
  and the Department of Defense (DoD)
- Remediation Technologies Development Forum, a
  partnership of the EPA, the DoD, and the Department
  of Energy (DOE)
- Air Force Center for Environmental Excellence
- Program Research and Development Announcements,
  EPA

The DoD and Air Force programs seem particularly attractive.
Their past operations have led to many sites contaminated with
gasoline and jet fuel. They seem quite serious about cleaning up
these sites and are interested in innovative ways to accomplish
the work.

Work Remaining
The work remaining includes gathering more information. I
am gathering detailed specifications for pipe construction and
installation. I am contacting the funding agencies to inquire
about their proposal procedures and the criteria they use in
judging proposals.

Page 4
Professor Mendoza
24 February 2000

When I have analyzed and organized the information, I will
prepare the first draft of the review in time to get it to you and
Professor Fuller by 22 March. Following the discussion with
you, I will have the final report to you by no later than 5 April.
I hope the review will be a well-documented summary of my
information that will be useful for your proposal.

Overall Appraisal
The library and Internet search has gone well. I have copious
notes that when analyzed and organized should be of great use
to you. The specifications for construction and installation of
steam injection pipes are quite detailed. Air Force funding
seems particularly promising.

cc. Professor William Fuller

Empirical Research Report

Appendix D comes from a journal called *Tree Planters' Notes* (48 [1997]: 12–17). As you read it, pay attention to the following aspects:

- The completeness of the abstract
- The way in which the literature review leads into both the research methodology and objective
- The clear statement of the objective
- The organization and detail of the Materials and Methods section (A fellow expert could easily replicate this experiment.)
- The use of appropriate headings
- The predominant use of passive voice in Material and Methods and active voice in Results and Discussion
- The use of figures to summarize and clarify data
- The explanation and emphasis of key data in the discussion
- The way in which the conclusions meet the stated objectives
- The system of documentation used

Thawing Regimes for Freezer-Stored Container Stock

Robin Rose and Diane L. Haase

Project leader and associate director, Nursery Technology Cooperative, Oregon State University, Department of Forest Science, Corvallis, Oregon

Three thawing regimes were applied over a 6-week period to frozen Douglas-fir (Pseudotsuga menziesii *(Mirb.) Franco.), western larch (*Larix occiden-talis *Nutt.), and ponderosa pine (*Pinus ponderosa *Dougl. ex Laws.) container stock: (1) rapid thaw followed by cold storage, (2) slow thaw, and (3) freezer storage followed by rapid thaw. Seedlings were outplanted to 3 sites in north-central Washington. A subsample of seedlings was evaluated for root growth potential (RGP) at the time of outplanting. Seedling performance was assessed after the first and second growing seasons. Although there were significant differences among species, thawing regime did not affect seedling growth or survival after 2 growing seasons nor did it affect RGP. The results indicate that seedlings can tolerate variations in thawing practices that may occur due to weather or other circumstances beyond control. However, it is noted that it may be best to keep seedlings in freezer storage for as long as possible in order to prevent storage molds.* Tree Planters' Notes 48 (1/2): 12–17; 1997.

Freezer storage of container seedlings, although an accepted practice in the nursery industry, is still a relatively misunderstood technique in some forest nurseries and reforestation organizations. Research and experience have shown that freezer storage can be a valuable management tool to a successful reforestation program. Freezer storage gives the nursery greater flexibility by allowing for lifting during late autumn and shipping the following spring. This results in a more balanced work load at the nursery and an effective "surge buffer" between nursery and field production (Hee 1987). Colombo and Cameron (1986) found that freezer storage of container black spruce—*Picea mariana* (Mill) B.S.P.—allows managers to safely delay budset of a late-sown crop, thereby reaching minimum acceptable height, without the risk of winter damage associated with outdoor storage. Furthermore, freezer storage is more suitable for periods in excess of 2 months, because carbohydrate depletion and storage molds can be a problem with long-term cold (2°F) storage (Ritchie 1982, 1984).

Freezer storage is often necessary to maintain crop dormancy when late-season planting is required in snowed-in units, especially for stock to be planted to high-elevation sites. Odlum (1992) noted that black spruce seedlings kept in frozen storage had greater subsequent root and shoot growth than those wintered outdoors, especially for those outplanted at a later date. Ritchie (1984, 1989) found that the rate of dormancy release in bareroot Douglas-fir—*Pseudotsuga menziesii* (Mirb.) Franco—seedlings was substantially retarded by freezer storage compared to those left in the nursery bed resulting in an expansion of the planting window and a higher, more uniform, physiological quality. Likewise, Lindström and Stattin (1994) found that freezer-stored seedlings of Norway spruce (*Picea abies* (L.) Karst.) and Scots pine (*Pinus sylvestris* L.) had a greater tolerance to freezing in the spring than those that were stored outdoors.

A concern with freezer storage is the thawing process. One thawing method commonly used is to allow the stock to thaw very slowly at temperatures just above freezing over a period of several weeks. Another method is to place seedlings in an area with ambient temperatures for several days prior to outplanting. The standard thawing practice for Weyerhaeuser nurseries is to spread seedling pallets out and allow them to thaw at ambient temperature (10 to 15°F) for 3 to 5 days (bare-root seedlings) and for 10 to 15 days (container seedlings) (Hee 1987). Whether thawed rapidly or slowly, field foresters prefer to have the stock thawed just prior to outplanting. However, changing weather conditions or other circumstances beyond control can result in thawed stock being held for several weeks in cold storage prior to outplant. Hee (1987) noted that it is best to plant seedlings as soon as they have thawed, but also noted that they can be held in cooler storage after thawing for up to 4 weeks without detriment.

The objective of this study was to examine the effects of 3 thawing regimes on the subsequent quality of 3 species of container-grown conifer seedlings outplanted to 3 sites. The thawing regimes were designed to simulate circumstances typically encountered with frozen stock. The null hypothesis was that there would be no differences in seedling field performance for any of the species due to thawing treatment.

Materials and Methods

Douglas-fir, western larch (*Larix occidentalis* Nutt.), and ponderosa pine (*Pinus ponderosa* Dougl.) container stock (1-year-old Styro-8) were used in this study. For each species on each outplanting site, seedlings were from the same seedlot. Seedlings were grown and freezer stored under standard nursery practices.

Seedlings were shipped frozen to the Leavenworth District of the Wenatchee National Forest in late March to early April 1995, depending on the expected date of planting for each site. Three thaw schedule treatments were applied over a 6-week period as follows:

1. Seedlings were placed under a rapid thaw (5 days at 7°C = 44.6°F) 6 weeks before expected outplanting, then held in cold storage (1°C = 33.8°F) until outplanting.
2. Seedlings were placed in cold storage for a slow thaw (6 weeks) before outplanting.
3. Seedlings were kept in freezer storage (–2°C = 28.4°F) until 1 week before outplanting, when they were placed under a rapid thaw.

Telog temperature recorders (Model 2103, Telog Instruments Inc., Victor, NY) were placed with seedlings in each thawing treatment. Because there were a limited number of Telogs available and because Telog data cannot be examined until it is downloaded to a computer, additional digital temperature probes were placed with the seedlings and monitored weekly.

Seedlings were outplanted to 3 sites on the Wenatchee and Okanogan National Forests in north-central Washington as follows:

- Twisp District, Okanogan National Forest; high-elevation (1,372 m = 4,500 ft) dry site. The slope is 10 to 40% with a northeastern aspect, with light slash and vegetation. All 3 species were planted on June 1, 1995.
- Leavenworth District, Wenatchee National Forest; low-elevation (610 m = 2,000 ft) dry site in area burned by 1994 wildfire. Annual precipitation is 53 to 76 cm (20 to 30 in). Soil is sandy to clay loam.

4 *Tree Planters' Notes*

The slope is 60% and the burned trees (avg. dbh = 10 cm = 4 in) were left standing. Douglas-fir and ponderosa pine were planted on April 20, 1995.

- Naches District, Wenatchee National Forest; high-elevation (1,219 m = 4,000 ft) temperate site. The slope is 15% with a western aspect. Douglas-fir and western larch were planted on May 31, 1995.

Seedlings were outplanted at about the same time that the site was scheduled to be operationally planted. Because of late-winter conditions, the 6-week thawing period was extended by 7 to 10 days for seedlings planted on the Twisp and Naches Districts. For each site, all seedlings were planted on the same day. Seedlings were planted at a spacing of 1.5 × 1.5 m (= 4.9 × 4.9 ft).

Initial height and survival were measured and recorded 2 weeks after outplanting and again at the end of the first and second growing seasons (September 1995 and August 1996). In addition, a damage/vigor assessment (incidence of browse, chlorosis, etc.) was recorded for each seedling.

In addition to the outplanted seedlings, a subsample of 15 seedlings of each species/treatment from the Leavenworth and Twisp sites were sent to International Paper's Lebanon facility shortly after seedlings were outplanted (that is, after treatment) and evaluated for root growth potential. These seedlings were potted and allowed to grow in a greenhouse for 3 weeks, then evaluated for the number of seedlings with new roots.

The experimental design consisted of a split-plot design with 5 blocks, 2 or 3 species per site (whole plots), 3 thaw treatments (subplots), and 10 seedlings in each block/species/treatment for a total of 450 seedlings on the Twisp site and 300 seedlings on the Leavenworth and Naches sites. All seedlings were labeled and randomly planted within a block.

An analysis of variance (ANOVA) was performed on all data to determine if thaw treatment has a significant effect on subsequent seedling performance. Differences among mean values for species and treatment were determined using Fisher's protected least significant difference procedure. Statistical Analysis Software (SAS Institute 1989) was used for all data analyses.

Results

It took about 5 days to accomplish the rapid thaw (treatments 1 and 3) and about 3 weeks for the slow thaw (treatment 2) (figure 1).

As would be expected, there were significant differences in field performance among species on each site (figures 2 and 3). However, there did not appear to be any meaningful differences among thawing treatments. During the first season, there were significant treatment by species interactions for both height and growth on the Leavenworth and Naches sites (figure 2). However, despite the statistical significance between treatments, the differences in first-year average height and growth may not be significant from a reforestation perspective, as the differences are small (1 to 3 cm = .4 to 1.2 in) and the ranking does not follow any pattern with regard to the treatments. For example, treatment 1 Douglas-

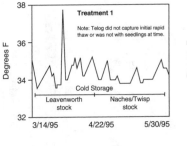

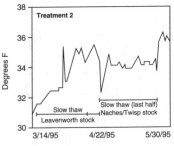

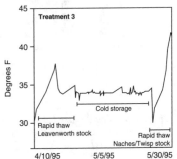

Figure 1—*Output from Telog temperature recorders showing the thawing process of each treatment.*

6   *Tree Planters' Notes*

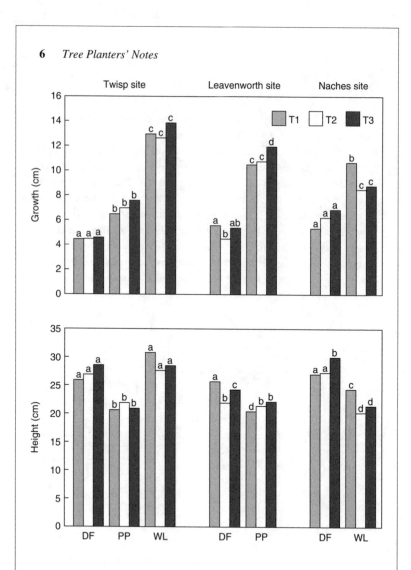

Figure 2—*Total seedling height and growth after the first growing season in the field (1995). On each site, bars with different letters are significantly different at the ∝ ≤ 0.05 level.*

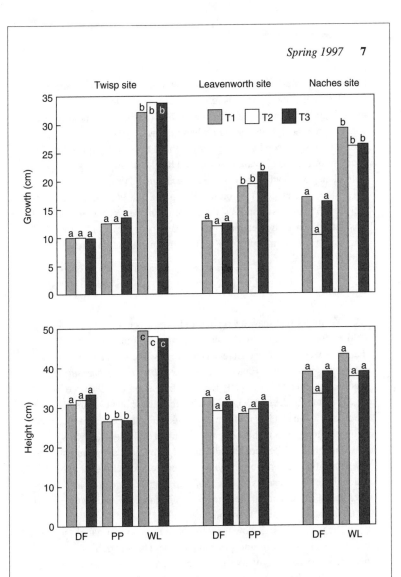

Figure 3—*Total height and growth after two growing seasons (1996). Although species differed significantly, there were no significant differences between thawing treatments. On each site, bars with different letters are significantly different at the $\propto \leq 0.05$ level.*

8   *Tree Planters' Notes*

fir had the greatest height on the Leavenworth site, whereas treatment 3 Douglas-fir had the greatest height on the Naches site. Similarly, treatment 3 ponderosa pine had the most growth on the Leavenworth site whereas treatment 1 western larch had the most growth on the Naches site. During the second growing season, there were no significant differences among thawing treatments for total height, seasonal height growth, or total height growth on any of the 3 sites (figure 3).

Survival averaged 77% on the Twisp site and 96% on the Leavenworth site regardless of species or treatment. On the Naches site, survival was not influenced by treatment but was very poor for Douglas-fir (23%) compared to western larch (83%). Thaw treatment had no effect on root growth potential.

Discussion

We found that thawing regime did not affect subsequent seedling field performance. In a similar study, Camm and others (1995) reported that there were very few differences between white spruce (*Picea glauca* (Moench) Voss) and Engelmann spruce (*Picea engelmannii* Parry) seedlings planted either directly from the freezer or after 9 days of thawing. The latter broke bud 3.3 days earlier than those planted directly from the freezer but had a less uniform budbreak. Height, shoot, and root mass did not differ after 3 months of growth. Camm and others (1995) suggest that a suitable on-site operational protocol for rapid thawing might be to lay frozen bundles on the ground at ambient temperature overnight. Additional possible benefits to this approach that they mention include reductions in handling costs, secondary storage facilities, and losses caused by refrigerator failure (Camm and others 1995).

The idea of a long, slow thaw has been to allow normal physiological processes to fully resume prior to planting. However, this may not be necessary because recovery of water potential after thawing spruce seedlings took hours, not days, once ice crystals left the roots (Camm and others 1995). As a result, these authors recommend against the practice of slowly thawing seedlings for up to several weeks before shipping to the plantation site because fungi (*Botrytis* spp.) often proliferate on seedlings held above freezing in the dark for extended periods. Another study showed that steady-state respiration rates increase significantly during thawing and hence have the potential to greatly deplete carbohydrate reserves, especially over time (Lévesque and Guy 1994).

On the other hand, Odlum (1992) stated that rapid thawing of stock can result in damage or mortality attributable to shoots rapidly rising to ambient thaw temperature, while seedling plugs remain frozen, due to their higher water content. Thus, foliar transpiration without water availability from the roots results in desiccation. Odlum recommended that stock be thawed slowly as described by Koistra and others (1989); seedlings are first exposed to 5°C until completely thawed. Our findings do not suggest the need for this.

Conclusions

Despite assertions in the literature of damage to seedlings caused by either rapid or slow thawing, the results of our study indicate that container seedlings can withstand variations in thawing regimes, as we described, without any detrimental effect to their subsequent field performance. However, managers concerned with post-storage fungal infection should consider using short thawing intervals.

Literature Cited

Camm EL, Guy RD, Kubien DS, Goetze DC, Silim SN, Burton PJ. 1995. Physiological recovery of freezer-stored white and Engelmann spruce seedlings planted following different thawing regimes. New Forests 10: 55–77.

Colombo SJ, Cameron SC. 1986. Assessing readiness of black spruce container seedlings for frozen storage using electrical impedance, oscilloscope square wave and frost hardiness techniques. For. Res. Note 42. Location: Ontario Ministry of Natural Resources, Ontario Tree Improvement and Forest Biomass Institute: 6 p.

Hee SM. 1987. Freezer storage practices at Weyerhaeuser nurseries. Tree Planters' Notes 38(2): 7–10.

Koistra C, Ostafew S, Lukinuk I. 1989. Cold storage guidelines. Victoria, BC: British Columbia Ministry of Forests.

10   *Tree Planters' Notes*

Lévesque F, Guy RD. 1994. Changes in respiration rates of white spruce and lodgepole pine seedlings during freezer storage and thawing and relationship to carbohydrate depletion. Poster presented at Annual Meeting of the American Society of Plant Physiologists. Portland, OR. July 30–August 3, 1994.

Lindström A, Stattin E. 1994. Root freezing tolerance and vitality of Norway spruce and Scots pine seedlings: influence of storage duration, storage temperature, and prestorage root freezing. Canadian Journal of Forest Research 24: 2477–2484.

Odlum KD. 1992. Maybe or maybe nots of frozen storage. Paper presented at OTSGA container workshop, 1991 October 1–3; Kirkland Lake, ON. Location: Ontario Tree Seedling Growers Association and Ontario Ministry of Natural Resources.

Ritchie CA. 1982. Carbohydrate reserves and root growth potential in Douglas-fir seedlings before and after cold storage. Canadian Journal of Forest Research 12: 905–912.

Ritchie GA. 1984. Effect of freezer storage on bud dormancy release in Douglas-fir seedlings. Canadian Journal of Forest Research 14(2): 186–190.

Ritchie GA. 1989. Integrated growing schedules for achieving physiological uniformity in coniferous planting stock. Forestry 62 (Suppl.): 213–227.

SAS Institute. 1989. SAS/STAT User's Guide, Version 6, Fourth ed. Cary, NC: SAS Institute. 846 p.

Chapter Notes

Chapter 3

[1]Adapted from Rebecca D. Williams, "FDA Proposes Folic Acid Fortification," *FDA Consumer* May 1994: 13.

[2]Adapted from Dick Karsky, "Scarifiers for Shelterwoods," *Tree Planters' Notes* 44 (1993): 14.

Chapter 4

[1]Nyle K. Walton, "Demographic Issues, *Geographic and Globaal Issues* Autumn 1993: 10–11.

[2]Mark Gerstein and Cyrus Chothia, "Proteins in Motion," *Science* 10 Sept. 1999: 1683.

[3]Gil Lambany, Mario Renaud, and Michel Beauchesne, "Control of Growing Medium Water Content and Its Effect on Small Seedlings Grown in Large Containers," *Tree Planters' Notes* 48 (1997): 49.

[4]Kenneth E. Trenberth, "The Extreme Weather Events of 1997 and 1998," *Consequences: The Nature and Implications of Environmental Change* 5 (1999). http//:www.gorio.org/consequences/vol5no1/extreme.html (5 January 2000).

[5]Adapted from Trenberth.

Chapter 5

[1]Updates, *FDA Consumer* 4 (1999): 6.

Chapter 7

[1]For an extended look at the ethical principles discussed in this chapter, see R. John Brockmann and Fern Rook, eds., *Technical Communication and Ethics* (Washington, DC: Society for Technical Communication, 1989). In particular, see H. Lee Shimbergs's "Ethics and Rhetoric in Technical Writing," 59–62.

[2]The Online Ethics Center for Engineering and Ethics http://onlineethics. org/(12 January 2000).

[3]For an excellent discussion of the principles discussed in this section, see Edward R. Tufte, *The Visual Display of Quantitative Information* (Cheshire, CT: Graphics Press, 1983) 53–87.

Chapter 8

[1]Adapted from Martin D. Tomasi and Brad Mehlenbacher, "Re-Engineering Online Documentation," *Technical Communication* 46 (1999): 55.

[2]Ricki Lewis, "Surprise Cause of Gastritis Revolutionizes Ulcer Treatment," *FDA Consumer* 28 (1994): 18.

[3]*The Chicago Manual of Style*, 14th ed. (Chicago: The University of Chicago Press, 1993) Chapter 16.

[4]Janice R. Walker and Todd Taylor, *The Columbia Guide to Online Style* (New York: Columbia University Press, 1998). Also available online at http://columbia.edu/cu/cup/cgos/idx_basic.html (20 November 1999).

Chapter 9

[1]David L. Wenny, "Calculating Filled and Empty Cells Based on Number of Seeds per Cell: A Microcomputer Application," *Tree Planters' Notes* 44 (1993): 49.

[2]The fusion energy argument is based on two sources. *About Fusion Energy*. http://wwwofe.er.doe.gov/More_html/About%20Fusion.html (18 January 2000) and *Fusion and the Environment*. http://wwwofe.er.doe.gov/More_html/environment.html (18 January 2000).

Index

Note: Bold numbers indicate pages with illustrations.